D0001703

I LOST MY JOB AND I LIKED IT

30-DAY LAW-OF-ATTRACTION
DIARY OF A DREAM JOB SEEKER

LILOU MACE

Published by Juicy Living Publishing 2009

First published in 2009 by Juicy Living Publishing

www.LilouMace.com

ISBN 978-0-9562546-0-3

This book is dedicated to you.

May you find your passion
and your true purpose in life.

Remember: You are the co-creator of your life!

ACKNOWLEDGEMENTS

I want to express my deepest gratitude to everyone I have met on my journey. You have inspired me to be the person I am now, and to want to make a difference to the lives of others.

I want to acknowledge my mom, Irene Martin, and my dad, Jean-Yves Mace, for giving me every opportunity in life. They equipped me with a solid education, a strong work ethic and dual citizenship. Thank you for your support, words of wisdom, prayers and unconditional love.

I want to thank Laura Duksta and Sandy Grason for lifting me to new heights, and for having joined me in launching the '100-Day Reality Challenge'. I have learnt so much from you ladies, and feel blessed to have met you and to have founded this incredible project with you. Your determination to succeed, to create ever more possibilities, and to spread love and creativity in this world, has been a constant joy.

I want to thank the entire CCOR '100-Day Reality Challenge' community – each and every member – for your love and support. You are my rock. I love you guys.

Big thanks to all my YouTube fans, for watching my videos, and for sending so many wonderful and supportive comments!

I want to thank my Scottish friend and editor, Dr R Eric Swanepoel, for helping me to put this book together in under six weeks. It has been a fun and flowing experience. Eric, you are gifted in many ways, but I particularly want to thank you for your commitment, integrity and creativity. You are a champion. I am so thankful that you have been part of this project. Your editing has taken the book to another level, while keeping my vision intact. You even kept me on track when it was needed!

I also want to acknowledge the talent of an amazing young man, who has shown both talent and professionalism. Jack Latimer, you have a great career as a photographer ahead of you, and I would say probably as a filmmaker too! Your creativity and passion are contagious. Thank you.

I want to thank Marc Holland for his creative genius in designing the cover and branding material. Marc, you are the most talented graphic designer I have met, and I love your way of thinking. Thanks also to Gerry Hillman, for designing the pages of this book, and for working under the pressure of tight deadlines. You made it possible under circumstances that were not ideal.

I want to thank my two wonderful London flatmates, Giada Vaghi and Henrik Vendelbo, for your support, long conversations, and the delicious nurturing that you offer my soul.

And I thank all my friends around the globe. In particular, my soul mate, Daniel Moore, for teaching me unconditional love, and believing in me when I had doubts. Also Hank Andries, for being such a playful champion and a great adviser.

Thanks also to Valerie Juillet, Isabelle Poucet, Cecile Madelenat, Nathalie Bonnard-Grenet, Celine Procop, Erhan Sakaoglu, Bryan Gutraj, Julien Bousquet, Sandra Gasnier, Mark Woodburn, Christelle Caron, Chantal Giroudon and Amarun, for their guidance, support and advice wherever I have found myself in the world. I want to thank my childhood friend, Geraldine Besse, who now lives in Brighton, and Peter Gould, my former boss, for bringing me to the UK. I am grateful, Peter, that you fired me. None of this would have happened without you!

I want to thank Oprah Winfrey for inspiring me to go for my dream, Kevin Ross for helping me create a vision, Tony Robbins for teaching me how to reach beyond my limited mind, and all the authors I interviewed on television and on the Internet. Thank you, John Beck and Elena Katardhieva, for your voluntary support in producing and filming the *My Juicy Life* TV show in Chicago.

Again I wish to thank everyone mentioned in this book who has been part of this quest to discover my dream job and to feel free again.

And, finally, I want to thank Life. I want to thank Life from all my heart, for the flow of abundance, creativity and joy that this project has brought me.

INTRODUCTION

My mission is to help you have a juicy life – not just any old life, but a life you feel passionate about, one that is *on purpose*, one that feels great! I want you to wake up in the morning and say: 'I cannot wait to see what Life will bring me today!'

I want to help you turn hard times into good times. Having lost my job I can fully empathise with others suffering at this time of economic hardship, and I feel better equipped to help them.

I am grateful that I have been practising the use of these various tools (mainly the Law of Attraction) for many years now. I am grateful that I started the '100-Day Reality Challenge' community (also known as 'Co-Creating Our Reality' or CCOR) in 2005 with Sandy Grason and Laura Duksta, two wonderful and amazing women who, having written respectively *Journalution* and *I Love You More*, are now famous authors in the self-development industry.

Over the last eight years I have come to realise the extraordinary creative power that we all have. I have posted hundreds of videos and blogs on YouTube (well over 400 to date) and elsewhere on the Internet, and I have observed my life unfold while applying practices such as taking 100% responsibility, visualisation, vision boards, healthy eating, brainstorming, participating in seminars, etc. I have been practising these techniques consciously and deliberately for over 1,000 days (in ten 100-day challenges, which I shall explain later) such that I feel I am now fully equipped to use them in facing the personal challenge that I have been given: the loss of my job.

I realise that not everyone has the tools that I have. Many people are frightened. Many are wondering, 'How can I get through this?' It is my duty and my mission to help *you*. So I will be sharing my journey. It will unfold though the pages of this diary and, hopefully, it will help you see how you too can manifest your dream job, or, if you do not want to call it a 'dream job', at least a job which, every day, stimulates the flow of new ideas, a job such that you feel you are making a real and valued contribution, a job that you do not simply tolerate or endure for the sake of survival, or even for the sake of having money to enable you to do the things that you love.

I hear people say, 'Get a good bed, you spend a lot of time sleeping!' Yes, we do, but we also spend a lot of time at work and we all have work. This book is most definitely *not* about finding *any* kind of work, but about finding work that is fulfilling.

Through this book you will follow the journey of someone – me – who is determined to find a fulfilling job, a job that makes me happy. My intention is to be outstandingly creative in this job, to have new ideas flowing in, to be part of a talented team, to make a difference, and to feel content. That is my desire, my intention and the context in which I am living my life.

UNPRECEDENTED NEWS

This afternoon I received a call from Peter Gould, the CEO of my company: 'Lilou, I have bad news.' He paused for a few seconds. It seemed an eternity. I had felt the tension in the company, and sensed something bad was about to happen, but nothing could have prepared me for his words: 'Your job is being made redundant. We're not going to be able to keep you any longer.'

My heart was pounding. I asked, 'So when do you want me to leave?'

He replied, 'Well, as long as you hand in all the work you have, and do a professional handover, you can leave now.'

In a few seconds, with those few words, my life changed. My future had altered. What was I going to do? I'd been in the job for six months – Internet Marketing Director for a London-based hospitality company. For the previous seven years I had worked in the USA on a self-employed basis. I'd applied for this job from the USA. I was thirsty for a new adventure. I was thrilled, and accepted the position. It's a dynamic, entrepreneurial company, but I have to say that it wasn't all plain sailing, especially the last few weeks...

I just accepted the news at face value, trying not to read too much into it. I stayed professional on the phone, and tried to find out more about the practicalities. 'OK, so how does this work? This has never happened to me.' Since I had been with the company for only six months, the official policy was to give me only a week's severance pay. However, as I had relocated from the USA, Peter told me that I'd be given a month's salary. I thought that was generous, and it was some relief. Peter told me to call Alexis, the HR person, to arrange the details. Before our conversation ended, I asked him to email the 60 employees working in the office to let them know immediately.

He sent an email explaining that I was 'moving to pastures new'. Pastures? What is that now? Is this a British way of saying that you have been sacked? I didn't think so. I had been fired and that was the truth, but that's not how he put it. He possibly meant to imply that things would be greener for me on the other side…? Yes, that was probably it… I was hopeful.

I was certainly grateful for that smooth and considerate email, as I did not want to be the recipient of everyone's sympathy, to look bad in front my colleagues. I had only worked six months in the position. Thirty minutes later, HR was in my office, and we discussed the details of my redundancy.

So that's the news today: I've lost my job.

All afternoon colleagues came into my office and asked me what I was up to. They wanted juicy details. Under pressure, I started making up a story that I had some plans that I could not, as yet, share, but, yes, I was certainly moving to 'pastures new', as Peter had said. All the while, as I was saying to people, 'It's been a great experience, but, you know, it's time to move on…,' I was thinking of what exactly these pastures could be. By the end of the day, having received numerous visitors and emails, a new scenario *was* taking shape in my heart and mind: I was inviting my life to lift off. The bad news was transmuting into great news. I felt increasingly liberated by the minute. Here was an opportunity for something new, an opportunity for something great to start. It was up to me.

I'm back home now, digesting the fact that I was made redundant today. This is a first. I cannot explain why I now feel such relief! It has awakened such joy in me – and energy. I look forward to being guided rapidly to something new and fulfilling, where I can truly develop my passions and purpose, and prosper to the fullest extent.

I have to admit that I was not happy at work and it was affecting my entire life, especially the last few weeks, always stressed, working long hours, sleepless and not feeling like the captain of my own ship. Yuck! But I have learned a lot there. I have sharpened my skills, but most importantly I have learned what I did not want. I am extremely grateful for that.

Now it is time for more – to find something new. I am asking Life to guide me. This is the time for my dreams to become real...

I LOVE AVOCADOS

It's three days since I lost my job, and I'm just doing what feels good, from moment to moment.

I am in the kitchen now. It is time to nourish my body. I am a raw vegan. For me, the main thing is to eat foods that feel good. For example, I love avocado. I am holding an avocado right now, and I definitely want to add it to this beautiful healthy salad I am about to create. I love the avocado's richness, its creaminess, and how it nourishes my body. So yummy!

NEW IDEAS FLOW

Soon after I lost my job I had the revelation that I should keep a journal as I look for a new job – a dream job – and then make this journal into a book. This project should help me and, I hope, others in this time of economic crisis. It should help them find what their true Selves really want!

I cannot believe how effortlessly the ideas have been flowing since then. I haven't stopped writing, whether on the London tube earlier, or now that I am in the kitchen trying to find the time to eat some healthy foods. I have all these amazing thoughts, attracting them one by one. I am really *aware* of this right now, and very, very grateful. This flow of ideas has been happening ever since I started asking for higher guidance.

AWARENESS

I am so struck by the fact that this is happening at such lightning speed! I have the thought that, yes, it *is* going to happen pretty fast, and, yes, I *am* going to get a book out of it. It is amazing to be riding that wave right now and my goal is to keep on feeling that way, to stay tuned and to feel guided. I am going to focus on anything that feels good. I am recording every single step, because every step now is important, as my life unfolds.

MY DIFFICULTIES WERE MEANT TO BE

I think people need this book *now*. People are losing jobs. Many are unhappy in their current positions. I wasn't happy in mine. I stayed there six months. I had a lot of conflict internally: learning how to deal with other people and teams, working with women... (Yes, I am one, but that doesn't make it easy!) So when I got the news that I had been sacked I was grateful because I had some understanding of the Law of Attraction. I knew this was not a coincidence; it was meant to happen.

And now, a few days later, I understand that there is something important unfolding. I must share this story to inspire others going through similar experiences, those who might not have the tools that I have acquired over the last eight years. So this book is to share my life with people who really need this support right now. It could be a guide to help job seekers, job haters, graduates, stay-at-home moms, and people simply bored with their jobs, not just to find 'a job' but *the* job, one that corresponds with their desires and needs, so that they can wake up in the morning, fully alive and passionate about what they are doing: a job they know that they do well but which stretches them, one that feels *great*! That is the kind of job I am talking about.

URGENCY

I feel a sense of urgency, because people are in real need. I feel compelled to share this journey – every single step – and the faster it happens, the sooner the book can go out, the better. I do not think I am the fastest typist but I can do a pretty good job. As yet, though, I'm undecided whether to transcribe the memos I'm recording myself, or attract somebody else to type them up.

A PRECEDENT: NEALE DONALD WALSCH

I had heard about Neale Donald Walsch, and then I saw the movie of his life, *Conversations with God*, on DVD about a year ago. After losing a highly paid job, he also lost his friends and found himself on the street at about 50 years of age. He kept asking God, 'Please God, help me, help me, help me!' As I remember it, he was sitting on a sofa one day when he suddenly started to write. He could not stop writing. I feel exactly the same right now. Walsch said that his writing was inspired by God.

I am very surprised that, all of a sudden, this is just coming out, but I realise that it was in me. It was in me and it is just coming out because I have allowed it to come out. I have asked for guidance. I have asked for higher guidance and I am receiving it. So I can see where Walsch was coming from. I remember in the movie the pages and pages and pages flowing out. He just could not stop.

I remember vividly the moment when God tells him: 'I am not concerned about your worldly success, only you are. You are not to worry about making a living. True masters are those that chose to make a life rather than a living. Go ahead, do what you really love. Do nothing else. You have so little time. How can you think for a moment about making a living from something you don't like to do? That is not a living. That is a dying.'

NURTURING MYSELF AND MANAGING OTHERS' EXPECTATIONS

I am learning how to nurture my ideas and be in my own cocoon. I am confident of what I am doing right now, but whether it be my family, my current flatmate or friends, I am not sure that they are ready to hear about it. I have to be careful. I feel very strongly about this but it is not an everyday thing to announce boldly: 'I am going to follow my passion. I have always wanted to empower millions, and this is my time to do so. I know it is the right time.' Other people in my life might not be able to relate to this, so I am just going to move forward with confidence, and reassure them in my own way – not lie, as such, but simply tell them that I have a plan and that I am working on it.

DEALING WITH FEARS OF SCARCITY

I want to get a domain name for this project, but I have this notion of *not enough*, and I find myself thinking: 'Maybe I should secure a domain name right now.' I think this fear is coming from a feeling of scarcity: 'Perhaps an established author or somebody with better skills will put a similar book out, and maybe they will put it out faster, and then they will be the successful one.' I cannot believe that I am now envious of someone who doesn't even exist! Such feelings of envy and scarcity could sabotage things, so I need to cancel this thought.

I want my book to sell in millions. The timing is right, but I am wondering how I should deal with my fears. I have to remind myself that my experience is all part of a bigger picture, and that it is up to me to interpret it. I can make anything from this if I want to. The interpretation I put on being sacked is a big part of me manifesting a dream job. I tell myself that this had to happen. Feeling angry or resentful is not going to help me. Feeling afraid of not being able to pay the bills is not going to help me. All those fears are there. I have lost my job, and this is the only fact, though; I should not add anything to it. What I have a choice about is how I interpret it and what I am going to focus on. This is important, because what we focus on expands. That is the Law of Attraction!

ASKING FOR GUIDANCE

If things are becoming possible right now it is because of all my previous experiences. The pieces of the puzzle are, indeed, coming together all of a sudden; importantly, I am allowing them to come together. I am asking for higher guidance. I am aware of my own abilities, but I am still asking for it: 'How can I receive? I want to receive higher guidance. I want to receive higher guidance!' I keep on re-stating this.

SYNERGY

It is amazing that this project is flowing as quickly as it is right now. I am able to do it because of previous experiences, because I have an iPhone and because I am in London: I have the technology and the knowledge to make it happen now. I have a burning desire, as Wayne Dyer would say. I strongly want this to happen right now. I feel that nothing can stop me. The moment feels right. My business, marketing and technical skills have been sharpened over the last few years in the USA and the UK. Everything – where you are right now – is because of the entirety of your experience. The good and the bad. It is all part of a puzzle, and my story is unfolding in front of my eyes right now. It feels as if it all finally makes sense.

IT IS AFFECTING ALL OF US

I am clear that I lost my last job for a reason. And I believe it is probably to help you, not just to find any job, but a job you really want and that you will be passionate about. Such help is really needed on the planet right now, particularly the USA, which I am really concerned about.

...But the economic crisis is not just happening in the USA, it is happening in Japan, Australia, in the UK, in Europe, France... People I love are being affected, people all over the world. We are having to face reality. It is affecting all of us. This is happening to our neighbours, to our good friends the world over. We have the notion of time being limited, and finances being limited, and so we are scared, and I, personally, am frightened right now, as I am standing here recording this. But at the same time I feel very empowered. Again, I am grateful for this technology that is helping me share my unfolding journey.

LOSING YOUR JOB IS NO ACCIDENT

Where we are standing *right now* is because of everything that we have experienced before. If, like me, you have lost a job, then this can be the opportunity for something new and better. When looking beyond the fear, I can see a bright future for me and for you. How about if this is something that was needed for us to be happier and more fulfilled? How about if this were the exact experience we needed to find our dream job?

DISMISSING MY INNER VOICE

I can remember dismissing my feelings at work. I remember telling myself that perhaps I was feeling that way because I had been self-employed for the previous seven years. I thought that maybe it was because I was not used to working in a large team and delegating so many aspects of my work. I speculated that it might be because I was new to the UK. I thought I was not performing as well because I was not good enough. I started to lose confidence in myself. I was questioning all these things, but really I was not listening to this thing inside... to what some would call my inner voice... telling me that *this* was not *it*.

THERE ARE NO COINCIDENCES

Yes, I am very grateful that my boss fired me. When he told me that my job had been terminated I felt relief: a very good sign! I know that each of us reacts differently to this kind of event but, if you can, then please get to this place where you at least feel some sort of relief about where you are, a certain ease with your situation, or at least an understanding that there might be no coincidence here. If you are reading my diary or listening to it, it is because you were meant to. Our thoughts attract our reality. Negative thoughts might attract the lessons we need. Good thoughts attract the things we need to find fulfilment.

NOT FOCUSING ON MONEY CONCERNS

Peter told me: 'Your job has been terminated. You can leave today. We do not need you any more.' My ego was definitely shocked, but I accepted it, and he offered me money to tide me over for a month. I believe that this money is providing me with the cushion I need to move forward, and I do not feel under too much pressure even though London is very expensive. Yes, I am concerned about being able to pay the bills, but I choose not to focus on this. I choose not to focus on it because I know there is a plan; I know that it is no coincidence that this has happened. I feel that something bigger is happening. This feels like it is the way it is supposed to be.

11

A NEW CAREER DIRECTION

Hmm… I am an Internet marketer by profession, so I should look for Internet marketing positions… *No!* – I stop myself thinking that – I do *not* have to look for an Internet marketing job! I have always wanted to write a book. I have always wanted to do TV. I have always wanted to empower millions of people. And this is the time, right now, for me to do this. It is my time to step up and serve. Another job as an Internet marketer is not going to make me feel any better, far less fulfil me. I know that. I am good at it, but it is not my passion any more. It is not my purpose in life. Life is now calling me for more.

INTERRUPTED SALAD: 'SQUEEZING' THE MOMENT

I have been trying to make this salad for the past hour, and I have only cut an avocado, and had to stop five times. If you knew me you would know that I love food so much that there is just no way I would stop any other activity, and I am laughing at this thought. Right now I am just so fulfilled, I feel so content, I am not even hungry. I am going to eat because I love eating (I am French, after all!), but this is taking a long time. This might be the slowest salad I have ever put together, but, you know what? This flow of ideas is happening right now, and I must not interrupt it.

You have to seize and squeeze the moment, and if 'it' is coming out, whatever 'it' is for you, then be ready to do it anywhere. In the tube earlier, the same thing happened, and I missed three stops. I was walking around the underground and not finding my way because I was typing the various ideas on my iPhone. Things were just flowing. It started at the gym earlier today and has not stopped since. Anyway, I should get back to my salad…

SHARE YOUR UNIQUE KNOWLEDGE IN THE WAY THAT SUITS YOU

I am not saying that you should write a book, and that this is all about writing books and sharing knowledge in that format. What I am convinced of, however, is that we all have something unique to share and that this is of fundamental importance. Some of us write journals, which is very therapeutic. Others do blogs, to share their thoughts online with others, which is amazing. Then there are videos. I do many videos on YouTube and I just love it. To date, I have posted about 410 videos – diary videos – in which I have simply been relating, day by day, what has been happening in my life and I will continue with this, as it is part of my '100-Day Reality Challenge' (http://www.CoCreatingOurReality. com).

My point is that we should share our knowledge with others, in whatever format suits us, especially as technology now makes this easier. If it's in book format, it's in book format. If it is something else, it is something else. Look at artists – they express their uniqueness through their art. Some people express it in writing. I was not a particularly good writer, but I had to get out of that zone. I have tried several times in the last few years to write a book, but I guess the timing was off. Besides, I had always had a voice in my head telling me I could not write. …That English was not my first language and so I could not write a book in English. So many reasons were holding me back. But now, the time feels right, and I am ready, and I also feel the world is ready to hear this. This feels so good; I won't be stopped by fears about my writing. This is too important. I discovered that, for me, the best way to do this was to talk to this little device, standing here in my kitchen. This is what I have attracted to me, and this is what feels great. If I am in front of a blank white page… well, it just does not work for me.

So, whatever your passion is, whatever you are visualising, whatever you want to do, you might just want to consider focusing on what feels good and allowing it to 'happen'. Ask for guidance, and the right medium will come to you, and the right people. Try it out! Give it a shot!

NO CHOCOLATE SACRIFICE

On the very night I was made redundant I went to this raw food party for chocolate lovers organised by Peter Pure. I thought to myself, 'I am not going to cancel my plans just because of being fired!' and I am very happy that I went. That was a significant shift – right there, in that moment. We continue to shift things, moment by moment. I just decided, 'You know what? I am still going to go instead of starting the job-research right now.' I went and I met some great people. I had a really good time. I just love chocolate, and Peter was so knowledgeable, sharing all this information about nutrition and how important it is. That raw chocolate party made me feel good and helped me to align myself with my passion instead of focusing on the news and changes to come. I was not a victim. I made a shift in that moment, to honouring who I was. I thought: 'I deserve this. This is going to make me feel good. So this is the right thing to do. Why not treat myself? I did not do anything wrong. No time to punish myself. This is time for a living, for enjoying the pleasure of tasting chocolate sauce, and for meeting new people.'

NO EXCUSES: THE SYMBOLISM OF A BOX OF HERBAL INFUSIONS

Impressed by everything Peter Pure put in it, I bought a 'tea box' that night. There are ten infusions: Camomile (for relaxation), Pau d'Arco (anti-fungal), Echinacea (immunostimulator), St John's Wort (anti-depressant), Eyebright (to treat eyestrain), Ginkgo biloba leaf (to enhance intelligence, concentration and memory), Green Tea (anti-oxidant), Peppermint (stimulates the appetite and aids digestion), and Nettle (anti-inflammatory). All these are in this box. Yes, I was tempted not to buy it as I ended up spending £100, all in all – quite of a lot of money to be spending only a few hours after losing my job! But it felt right, and I am so grateful that I did buy this box and various other items because now, looking at all those little herbs that I have been infusing and drinking since this morning, I realise that they are giving me permission to live to my full potential. As human beings, we all have thoughts of not being clever enough, or of not having a good memory, and of feeling stressed. Really, these are excuses, and this tea box is helping me to avoid such traps because I am taking something to help me defeat them. You could say it is giving me 'an excuse' to fully express all my gifts all of a sudden.

YOUR INTUITION KNOWS BEST: WHAT FEELS GOOD?

Sometimes we find ourselves doing things that will go on to help us in unforeseen ways, for the simple reason that it feels good at the time. Although we do not necessarily work it all out logically in our brains, we register it on some level. I did not buy the box of tea at the time thinking, 'Oh, I have to do this in order to...' No, it was not an 'in order to'; it was a 'feel-good'. I bought the box because it felt right at that moment, and because I was interested in one of those herbs – Ginkgo biloba – because it is for brain and memory and intelligence, and I always had this thought, 'Oh, I have bad memory', and so I went ahead and bought the box. Now it is serving its purpose, it was part of the plan. I am glad I did not resist buying it!

TREAT YOURSELF TO WHAT MAKES YOU FEEL GOOD...

My major point is: don't stop *everything* because you just lost your job, or because there is an economic crisis, or because you have to be careful and make savings, or because you have maxed out your credit cards. I am not saying you should spend for the sake of it – if it does not feel good then *do not* spend – but I have just registered at a high-end gym in Kensington which costs nearly £100 more per month than my old one. It is a lot of money, especially at a time when you could say that I should be thrifty, but I am so grateful I did it. As I was out of a job, I knew I was going to have some spare time and I knew it was important to spend some of this as *quality time*. I wanted to make sure that I was going to be busy, in my mind's eye, and not just staying home alone, getting increasingly depressed. Instead, I would be finding ways to keep my morale up, and staying energized.

…ECONOMISE IN OTHER AREAS

However, I was more cost-conscious when I went to Whole Foods after registering at the gym. I picked up some organic avocados and bananas, but I did not go on and on shopping and buying the whole store, as I usually do. I was still very happy with my purchases, because this is the food I prefer. (If I had bought the whole store I would probably have felt bad afterwards.) The £49 that I shall pay at the gym for the rest of the month, pro rata, is probably what I saved through not buying unnecessary items at the store. I could have bought more, yes, but I did not really need those things as my fridge already contained some food. It would have been an extra expense, whereas investing in the gym… Yes, it is pricey, but it has a swimming pool and beautiful facilities. I feel so great every time I walk into it.

I used to go to the one in Regent Park next to work, but I never liked it, frankly. I dragged my feet there only one or twice a week. In Chicago, I went to East Bank Club, to this beautiful, awesome place where Barack Obama and Oprah Winfrey used to exercise, and still do when they are in town – 11,000 members, just the biggest club that exists, I think, in the entire world, if Dubai has not created an even bigger one! It was like a country club, absolutely amazing, and I missed that. It has taken me a bit of time to find my feet – six months now – and I feel so grateful that I have attracted this new gym and have not had to change my plans because I lost my job.

FORWARDS, NOT BACKWARDS

I am moving in ten days, to Earl's Court, and I was thinking that maybe I should reconsider… maybe go back to France, but I reflected: no, that would not feel good! I remember the time just after I left college when my mom was always on my case about finding a job. I don't blame her for anything but it led me to move to the USA, as I was thinking that *she* was responsible for me not finding a job. I thought: 'Better get out of the way and live life on my own, and then I will be able to find the job that I want.' But I do not want to do this a second time. I learned my lesson.

Don't get me wrong. I love my mom. She is the most precious thing I have in my life. She is simply amazing. I love her to pieces. She is the most loving, generous, elegant and social person I have ever met. But back then she was an obstacle. I was not fair to her, but life took me to the USA and it was an amazing experience.

…So, it led me to the United States and – no regrets – I lived there for eight years. I was self-employed. I had a ball. I met amazing people, like my best friend Daniel Moore who lives in Florida, and Hank Andries who now lives in Michigan. I met Oprah Winfrey who absolutely put me on track for living my passion. (She is someone I very much admire.) I was able to start a TV show there. I was able to start raw food and learn about so many things. I was able to put together seminars, meet Laura and Sandy with whom I co-founded 'Co-Creating Our Reality' and the '100-Day Reality Challenge', and I started to do my videos on YouTube. The United States was a wonderfully enriching experience.

None of this would have happened were it not for the clash between my mom and myself at the end of college. But right now, at 31, I do not think it will serve me well to go back to my parents. I am now an adult. I want to take full responsibility for where I am and where I am going.

I want to continue with my plans and move to Earl's Court in a couple of weeks. I feel great about my new place and about the amount of money I am paying to rent it. I am going to have faith that things are happening, and that I am going to be supported financially. I am keeping an abundant mindset. I also feel good about it because I have reserves to cope financially for a few months, so I am doing things responsibly as well. I think it is important to be responsible. Although I say it is important to stick with the plans that were created from a place – a state – of feeling good, I am not saying we should spend money and put everything on our credit cards and get into debt.

THE POWER OF DECLARATIONS

But this new place... I love it. It makes me feel so good just thinking about moving there. I am so happy to be moving very soon.

I had declared on video exactly the type of place I wanted, and it has all the things I described. It has the high ceilings, it has the big windows, it has the fireplace, it has a lot of space for cupboards, and it has the central location (not far from South Kensington) that I wanted. So I am moving forward. This is the physical place I attracted from the emotional place of feeling good This is the flat I manifested by simply stating exactly what I wanted, what it will look like, how it would feel. I had described everything about it. So, when I walked in, I knew it was it. I had only seen the front door, and I knew this was it. The rent was also what I was willing to pay, so I immediately said yes. My ex-flatmate was laughing at me for even considering that I could find such a place in London for that price, but I knew I would. I had my special Law-of-Attraction plan, the genie-in-the-bottle trick, to make a wish: 'Your wish is my command!' Boom! It appears. I just love it. I have so many Law-of-Attraction stories on my YouTube channel (youtube.com/liloumace), from how I met Oprah Winfrey to how I attracted $20,000, from how I attracted a cute convertible to how I landed new clients. It is all there. Check it out. If, at this point, you still doubt the power of consciously applying the Law of Attraction, then visit it immediately!

TIME FLIES WHEN YOU'RE HAVING FUN

I am done chopping the avocado and the red pepper but that's all. It is now 4 o'clock. Gee! Time is passing by, but this has been very productive and is very exciting.

LIFE AS A RECIPE

I think life is like a recipe. You put one ingredient in at a time. It felt good to add those avocados, and then the red peppers, and now I am adding basil, and I do not know what the final recipe will look like. But I know it will taste good and feel good.

It is the same in life. You just add one ingredient at a time. I think it is important not to be overwhelmed by thoughts like 'Oh, I need to get this right!' and 'Oh, what are the consequences if I do this?' Just go with the flow and add one ingredient at a time.

Concerning ingredients... I choose them, I feel them, and if they feel good in my hands, I chop them. If I feel an ingredient is going to nourish my body, and it will feel good once all of them are together, then I add it to the recipe. It is important to know what you want, but sometimes life unfolds and you must have faith. You might only be able to see what the next ingredient is, but you are still moving forward with the recipe! You do not stop there in the middle of it. You taste it. If it lacks a bit of salt then you will add salt, right? I feel it is the same in life! If you are at least committed to finding something that will feel great – a job that will match what you want – then things will come together for you, one step at a time. You are going to meet the right people and you are going to reach for the right ingredient and have a great recipe and a wonderful meal... a wonderful life.

PUT THOSE MUSHROOMS IN THE BIN!

When you are making a meal, as in life, you come across various potential ingredients, and not all are appropriate. For example, right now I am contemplating these mushrooms. Frankly, I've had them in my fridge for a while, and they were brown from the moment I bought them. Although I wanted to put them in this salad, every time I cut one of them it just did not feel right. These mushrooms might represent something that is about to arise, or has arisen, in your life, something that is rotten inside. It is not the right thing and yet you still put it in your salad, you still accept it. Well, I say: 'Take those mushrooms and put them in the bin.' If it does not feel right then there is no need to continue with it. Nobody is going to force you to eat those mushrooms, so put them in the bin!

Yes, we have been brought up to think of this as wasteful, but you know what it is a bigger waste? Not feeling good about yourself. This is how important you are to the world. You have a unique mission that no one else can fulfil. You have something unique to put out. Therefore, if you are doing something that does not feel good, you are taking something away from all of us. I want you to give this point your full consideration. Go and grab those rotten mushrooms that are happening in your life and, whether or not you have been eating them, put them in the bin right now!

TOUGH IS GOOD? GOOD IS TOUGH?

And then there are those hot peppers... I am thinking of adding this one to my salad – boy, this little baby is so hot my mouth will burn! But you know what? My salad needs a bit of spice, and this chilli pepper is going to stimulate, it is going to be good for me! It has lots of vitamin C. My point here is you might want to add some things that are going to be tough to take on, but you know how valuable and good they are going to be in your life in the long run. These are worth chopping up small and adding to your salad.

I am going to chop those pieces of hot pepper really finely; I am not obliged to cut them into big chunks. The same with life: those things that are harder to take on, but which you know are good for you and will result in good things, just cut them into smaller pieces, or divide your time and do them in smaller portions – going to the gym, for example. It does not feel easy right now, because I am out of shape, frankly, as I have not been exercising for a while, but I do know that I have to take the strain because it feels so good after each workout, and it is going to increase my confidence. The benefit is huge, so I am going to do smaller workouts and slowly build up.

CANCEL NEGATIVE THOUGHTS

You notice I said 'slowly build up'? Those are the words I just used. You should be very careful and watch what you say as this creates your reality. I was, in effect, saying that things are going to be slow; but then this becomes the context, the reality I am creating for myself. No! I am cancelling that thought. I say to myself 'Cancel, cancel!' and then I create something else because otherwise it stays there, that negative thought. And that's one thought that then leads to another thought, and then others... But I am on a high, on a roll... I want to attract, very quickly, this job of my dreams, and put this project together, so I am cancelling that thought.

THE RIGHT ENVIRONMENT FOSTERS CREATIVITY

You know what is even more interesting? All these thoughts are coming as I am preparing food, and, funnily enough, my dad is a chef and he himself wrote a book years ago, although it has never been published. (I guess it should be called a manuscript.) *The Art of Cooking Zen* is all about feeling the ingredients, and choosing the food depending on how you are feeling. It is about following your intuition, and letting your body's needs and your creativity take over! Dad is such a gifted chef, and maybe my ideas are flowing right now for the simple reason that I am in my natural environment. I grew up with him cooking and I am very close to food. …Or maybe it's simply a matter of being French! Whatever the explanation, I see every single one of those vegetables as a metaphor for some aspect of life. I am amazed.

ONE DOOR CLOSES, ANOTHER OPENS

At the gym earlier, I was exercising when ideas started to flow. Even more ideas were flowing after the workout – I was in my bathrobe, feeling relaxed and doing my hair, and all these thoughts were coming. So I panicked: 'Oh my God! I have to stop everything and start writing or grab a computer.' Then I remembered that there were a few iMacs at the gym, and I love Macs, so I assumed this would be perfect and I could simply type up my ideas on one of those.

I started on the first computer and it was slow. I started on the second, thinking it might be better because it was in a more secluded spot, but I could not figure out how to open Internet Explorer. I went to the third computer and it froze, and that was all three computers! It took me three computers before I figured out that this was not the right place and the right moment.

I tried to use my iPhone because the ideas were flowing so strongly, and started typing on it, using the notepad function. Not paying attention to where I was going, I kept stopping all over the underground, getting lost along the way.

Now, since I am back home and my flatmate is not here, I can use this recording device and simply record all my thoughts. I feel great about it. I feel really good talking to this device and expressing my thoughts like this. Paper does not work for me: the thought of the blank page put me off writing a book.

UNIQUE METHODS FOR UNIQUE PEOPLE

I remember Neale Donald Walsch wrote on a notepad, line after line after line, but for me this was not it. Sometimes you can get hung up on how other people do things. Don't feel you have to do things the same way as others. If necessary, embrace innovation and do things in an original way, in your own unique way.

We all have a unique way of doing things. If you try to do something new or find an idea and you go about it the same way as others, the results will be the same… or worse. The idea here is to fine-tune things and do what feels good for you. When you find that, then things just flow, as is the case for me right now with this recording device. Doing it this way feels amazing. I cannot believe I am being so chatty right now. It is coming together.

THE IMPORTANCE OF DREAMING (BIG!)

People sometimes say to me: 'Oh, you dream big. You are a dreamer. You dream too big.' Yes, I dream, but no, I don't see it as a fault; I think it is one of my biggest strengths. If I did not dream my life would be totally dull and boring. I do not envy anybody who simply exists, and thinks the old boring way, and never steps outside their comfort zone.

It is because I dream that I went to the USA. It is because I dream that I started my own business at the age of 24. It is because I dream that I dared to declare that I was going to meet Oprah Winfrey. It is because I dream that I met her in person, and she then inspired me to start my own TV show in Chicago. It is because I dream that I put together a volunteer team to run this show. It is because I dream that I am now in the UK doing this. It is because I dream that I am now sharing these thoughts with you. It is because I dream that this book will make a difference in your life. It is because I dream that I will help millions of people to live fulfilled lives. It is because I dream... It is because I dream... It is because I dream.

...AND THEN ALLOWING THE DREAMS TO HAPPEN

...And it is not simply because I dream, but also because I allow my dreams to happen, and I take actions that feel good, in line with these dreams.

We all have not just one but many dreams. We have some that are certainly more important than others, and dreams that grab us more.

UNLEASH YOUR 'POWER WITHIN'

I know I cannot be positive all the time, and I know I have my negative thoughts. Sometimes when I stick my neck out and declare my ambitions in public something inside of me is scared... You know that scary feeling? Some call it butterflies. You know exactly what I am talking about – when you get outside your comfort zone, and yet it feels good? The feel-good is on top of it? It does not feel 'bad', as such, but it is scary, it terrifies you!

This is exactly the direction that you could and should be taking right now, because it will lead to something even bigger.

If it were not for facing my fears then I would not have come this far in my life, I would not have been put myself on the spot in various ways, and have found myself enjoying every single second of challenging situations, and I mean fully enjoying them. I call it living a juicy life: a life of purpose and passion.

I remember the Anthony Robbins class that I did (Unleash the Power Within) back in Orlando a few years ago – especially the fire walk, and how we conditioned ourselves before stepping on the hot coals. We had to visualise ourselves on the other side of the sizzling embers, being happy to be on the other side. We had to celebrate our victory in advance. I remember the power move that he taught us, to pump our energy right up in seconds. And it worked! I was in awe at this exploit. I did not cheat; I conditioned myself, and I did it! It was an incredible, mind-blowing experience. I shall never forget that night, when I unleashed some of my 'power within'. I use the techniques of visualisation and energy boosting to this day, in interviews, auditions and meetings. Whenever I need to reach my peak potential. Like athletes, we can conditions ourselves to win.

WHAT FLOATS YOUR BOAT?

I just love the camera. There is something about the video camera, in particular – and not having anybody in front of me– that works for me. It might not work for others. I am not comfortable in front of 10,000 people, although one day I will be! I am terrified of public speaking. I have tried it many times. I do want to share my knowledge with millions of people but my outlet is not, for the moment, that of public speaking.

So what floats your boat? We all have our own 'things'. Think about what it or they might look like for you… about what feels good. Make a list in your journal of all the things that feel good in your life. For me it feels good when I am in front of the camera, it feels good when

I am on the Internet, it feels good to socialise, to travel, to organise events. It feels great to do video diaries. It feels great to say, 'I want to empower millions of people.' It feels right. It feels great to walk in nature, to go to the gym, to eat green food... List everything now! Go on and on.

THE RIGHT THING AT THE RIGHT TIME

Sometimes in life we are given things that we are not quite ready for. For instance, a book – you start reading it because people (or even myself) have recommended it to you: 'It helped her. I am going to get it and I shall learn so much from it.' Well, you know what? You might have that book in your hands – I am not talking about this particular book, as I am sure you are enjoying it! – but some other book... OK, even if it this is the book, if it is hard to read then just put it to one side and wait. If you are not enjoying it then leave it for now and go back to it later. One day it will feel right. I cannot even tell you how many books I have started and I have finished a month later, or two or six years later. I finish others in a day, in hours – it's the right moment, it's the right time for them. I hope this book is like that for you right now, that it feels right and that these words are exactly what you needed to hear. If that is the case, then I invite you to share it with others.

NEW WAYS OF THINKING URGENTLY NEEDED

The economic crisis is bringing us to the realisation that life is about collaboration, it is about helping each other; it is not about holding information back. We have to learn that, as human beings, we are very powerful. Everything is now being radically questioned because of the financial crisis. Old ways of thinking are collapsing and disintegrating. We have to re-learn what it takes to be a human, and how *we* should function. The moment is now!

YOU ARE SO ON TRACK!

I want to acknowledge you for picking up this book, because you are now at the cutting edge of thinking when it comes to what it is to be a powerful human being. The fact that you have come this far illustrates how things really work. You have taken a stand for yourself, or someone took one for you by giving you this book. Whichever one of these applies, the fact that you are reading it now suggests you have some hope that something different is possible. It is mind-blowing that you are here now. I hope you can also acknowledge yourself for this achievement. Wanting more is a big step. Claiming it is the second step, and then you shall receive!

WILL YOU JOIN ME?

More and more people are coming to this realisation – of how things work – and I want to ask you to be my partner in helping to spread the word. Perhaps when people receive this gift from you, or when you tell them about this book, their reaction will be 'What? I really don't get it!' or they might be enthused and start reading it, but not really do anything for a while. Nonetheless, they will have it. They may put it to one side and perhaps get back to it later, when the time is right. It is about being ready and wanting to receive this information.

I am not a believer in imposing anything on others. In the past, when I saw that someone was not interested in the Law of Attraction, I still imposed a conversation about it on him or her. Then I noticed that there are some people who are ready and some who are not. Now, with what I know and with the way I am moving forward in life, I have this knowledge – this thought – that I will be attracting people who want to learn more about it. These days I spot people in the London underground reading *The Secret*, or I tell by the way people speak to me that they are 'co-creating' their lives, as I call it. Those who are not yet ready will wake up one day. We each have a different story, a different timing.

SALAD FIRST, THEN MOM

I just had my mom on the phone and she wanted a good chat. I look forward to talking to her, but right now I need to feed this body. It's OK to say no, even to the people you love. I think it is as important in life to say YES as NO; sometimes NOs are even more important! They will understand, as long as you are open about it. Be a human being and say what is going on. So right now I am going to focus on eating my salad before my mom calls back.

Right now I need to eat, to nourish this body, and do this recording, before I talk to my mom. She said, 'In 10 minutes, no more.' And I said 'OK, Mom!' You have to know what you want. When she calls me back I am going to be fully present with her. Remember to take some time for yourself and learn how to say no. It is OK to say no.

People have their own agenda. It is ultimately about them, no matter what they say, so they can interfere in your life – your husband or brother, your mother-in-law or your boss. They impose their own stuff on you and you are going to have to be rock solid in insisting that you need your own time and that you need to give priority to yourself sometimes. I am not saying don't help others. Be there for others, by all means, but first you have to build into your life what you need.

THE POWER OF INTENTIONS

It is funny how they come over all worried about you: 'What is going on? You have not eaten yet! Is there a problem?' So now Mom is going to interrogate me because I told her I just got fired. She is going to ask me all those questions like 'What happened? How are you going to get by?'

STOP! I need to state an intention before talking with her.

This is a very powerful technique. You can create a context for meeting people, for instance. You can create a context for your life, or for a season of the '100-Day Reality Challenge'. I am in Season 11 right now, and I created the context of my life being 'juicy', so anything that is not 'juicy' is ruled out. This is a short way of saying that I want to have *fun*, to live *on purpose* and *with passion*. My season is definitely about being juicy – as you can no doubt tell from what's happened so far – and I am sure even juicier things are about to happen!

Anyway, my intention with my mom is to have a lovely conversation. I want her to have this deep 'knowing' that I have things under control.

COMING OUT

I am not going to tell her about me writing a book, because this is not going to help my case. I prefer not to talk about it, as she always says that I am a dreamer. I have to choose with whom to share my dreams.

I did tell Paul, a guy I met only recently, that I had been fired. I 'came out'. I needed to have a conversation with a near-stranger at first; I did not need a friend. Friends want the best for you – yes – but sometimes their concern can be expressed in unhelpful ways; they mean to do well, but they want to protect us, and it's not always appropriate.

I am a believer in coaches, in getting professionals to help, because they are impartial. I felt bad about losing my job and it was easier to start saying it to a stranger. I co-founded a community with thousands of members, and I felt bad thinking that I lead this community and here I am losing my job. I had to make a conscious decision to take it out there.

…But I am still afraid to tell my friends. It does not feel good. The more people I let know about this, the more likely it this that I shall end up feeling 'poor me', feeling like a passive victim: 'Oh poor you, you are out of work! Oh, yes, you were uncomfortable in your last job. I understand.' Such negative stuff can build. I am just not quite ready for this.

DO NOT DENY YOUR EMOTIONS, BUT DO NOT LET THEM RUN YOU

On the other hand, you have to experience things fully. If you are sad, then cry. If you are angry, be angry. Do not pretend those emotions are not there. Fully live them. And then you can learn how to shift your energy, by going to the gym, for example. But do not pretend things are all right. If you are upset and feel like crying then fully express that. Those are normal human feelings. It might mean that you need to go away for couple of days, to spend some time on your own in a natural environment with a good book and a journal. Take some time for yourself, the time you need. We all have a different story and react to things in different ways. But don't let the story run you too long. Being a victim in life – blaming others – doesn't work. Have you noticed? We can only really change ourselves. Being 100% responsible for how our lives are turning out – good or bad – is to me a major first step in starting to creating a juicy life, a fulfilling life, full of adventures, playfulness and joy.

LIFE CAN BE MAGICAL, IF YOU WANT IT TO BE

When I got the news, I knew that it was no coincidence. I am not one of life's victims. I am 100% responsible. If I am not feeling good, then I know I need to change something. In this case my boss helped me make that change. I did not have the guts to quit when I knew this was the thing to do. The way it happened was the best way it could have happened at the best time. Things just work out. There is magic to life if you want there to be. Everything that is happening to you was meant to happen that way. Immediately after traumatic events is not the time to over-analyse what happened. It is a time for feeling good (once you have expressed your emotions), and for aligning yourself to your true Self, a time for taking things one step at a time.

THE FRUSTRATION OF A CLOSED DOOR

There are some things that you really want to happen, but they are not happening. You are faced with a closed door, and you keep on trying and trying to open it, but it just won't budge. Now, I don't believe that because things didn't happen in the past they won't happen in the future, far from it. But maybe the timing is off. So, if you keep insisting on getting a particular job, and it is not working, then maybe that door is not suppose to open; there might be something else.

In the context of moving forward and feeling good, because we are on this planet to have a good time and life is short... (Actually, I should cancel this thought: cancel, cancel! Life is long... eternal!) In the context of moving forward and feeling good... if the door stubbornly remains closed then don't force it. Move on.

RELEASE THE OARS AND DRIFT DOWNSTREAM

To use another metaphor here, you can think of people's lives as rowing boats in a river. Esther and Jerry Hicks in their books (which I really love), *Ask and It Is Given* and *The Astonishing Power of Emotions*, describe it really well. Most of us are struggling to row upstream. We fight the current and we work hard. This is how we are raised. This is how we grew up: 'You have to work hard to get to what you want!' So the notion exists that this is the only way things can work. But things do *not* have to be hard! Release the oars. Try to picture yourself in the river right now. Close your eyes and see yourself going upstream with everything that is happening in your life: your boss – your *angry* boss – your co-workers, and everything like that… everything that was or is happening. Try to see how 'upstream' you were, fighting the current all the time. Working hard. This does not feel good, does it? Well, now your oars have been released for you. Or, if you are still in a job, and not enjoying it, you can release the oars and your work can transform. Yes, I am not saying you have to quit your job if you are in a position that you like, but release the oars and see what happens. Stop fighting. Your life will not be better upstream. There is nothing upstream that you want and fully desire. You are not going to be fulfilled in that direction. If you release those oars, you will flow down with the current and things will start happening, magically and effortlessly.

'ANCHORING' GOOD MOMENTS

Yum, yum…! This salad, that I made with my heart, choosing only the ingredients that felt right, feels so good. There are times in your life when you select the right ingredients and feed your body with the right food, when you have good thoughts and choose the things that make you feel really good. Remember a moment in your life that felt like that. I am sure you can find it, whether it was at your wedding or when you where a kid. Remember it. Write what you remember in your journal. When you have done this, close your eyes, and fully re-live that moment for a minute or two. Re-feel it. Then I want you to press your thumb and index finger together. This will 'anchor' that beautiful and strong feeling. Next time you do not feel so good, just press those two fingers together again and the feeling will come back. This is a very powerful technique.

VISUALISING HAPPINESS AND SUCCESS

If you have a moment, try a second quick, yet powerful, exercise. Imagine yourself in a new job that you fully enjoy, or imagine things working out for you in some other way. Close your eyes and live that for two minutes. If you are not sure what the details will be, at least feel it. See yourself walking in the street, happy, or having excited conversations with people you know. You are feeling so good about what is happening for you. It would be great if you could do this at the beginning of every day. This will set the tone for the day. I guarantee that your day will go more smoothly; you will be more creative and more present.

KEEPING A 'GRATITUDE JOURNAL'

Do you want to hear another of my little tricks? At the end of every day take your journal and list all the things that happened on that day for which you are grateful, whether it was for a good meal, for a conversation, or for having met a stranger who made you smile. You will soon realise how things are just putting themselves together for you. Some people might prefer to write a blog so they can share it… or make a video. It's not important. What is important is that this gratitude journal – in whatever format – is a piece of the puzzle that is coming together for you now, and I promise you that it is amazing. The phone is ringing now. My mom is calling back…

REASSURE YOUR LOVED ONES

It went well with my mom. I managed to reassure her that my life was on track and that I had a plan. She did not ask for details. I shared with her how things were emotionally. It was honest and straightforward. It went really well.

THE IMPORTANCE OF CREATING AN INTENTION

You can always choose what you want to share; you do not need to tell it all. I did, however, share with my mom the news that I lost my job. I did not tell her that I enjoyed the fact as much as I do, and that I was writing a book.

Her response was: 'Find something that you love.'

This was a turning point. In the past I would have expected her to say something like: 'There's an economic crisis. You should be focused on finding a job, and you certainly can't afford to be choosy about it. Get a job – anything you can.'

So what made her respond differently this time? I had created a different context. I approached her differently. She could hear in my voice, then, that I was confident of myself – that I was going in the right direction – and she responded accordingly.

This positive experience is now contributing to my enthusiasm, encouraging me to immerse myself completely in the flow.

I feel good. I am reconnecting with myself right now.

TECHNIQUES FOR SHIFTING ENERGY

When a conversation takes an uncomfortable turn – for example, when you upset someone because they do not understand your point of view – it's useful to know how to shift energy. There are several techniques and practices you may find useful.

Breathing

One thing you can do is simply stop everything and breathe deeply, in and out. Just focus on that. Taking time out like this will help because sometimes when we are stressed we do not breathe properly; our breaths are short and shallow. So whether you are at work or not – wherever you are – just concentrate on breathing, in and out. If you feel the need for privacy then by all means go to the toilets. Perhaps, if you stay there for ten minutes, people will think you are constipated – ha, ha! – but at least you will have some time and space to yourself! Remember: simply breathe deeply, in and out. You can do this quietly; it does not have to make any noise.

Journals

Anything that feels good will help you shift energy. If you are at home, or it is handy, you can write a journal, and make a note of whatever you are feeling and thinking. This is particularly useful if you are angry or upset and you feel the need to let it out. Do so! Take that journal and, if you are not entirely comfortable with your situation, or you have certain concerns or worries, start writing down everything that is bothering you. If you want to learn more about this I encourage you to read Sandy Grason's (http://www.SandyGrason.com) book *Journalution*. You will learn how to journal and, if you do this already, how to take your journaling techniques to an entirely new level.

I must emphasise that shifting your energy is not about *pretending* that everything is OK. That is emphatically not what I am talking about. I am not talking about positive thinking; I am talking about feeling good and being fully responsible for what is happening in your life. This is a place of power, of 'empowerment'. If you do not feel good then you are not going to make the right decisions. The priority is to feel great, and that will lead to you being inspired, meeting someone, doing something that will create unexpected results... Your job is to act when things feel right; just follow that inner guidance.

Vision boards

Another technique for shifting energy is to create a 'vision board', which are simply collages of what you want to attract in your life. They are very powerful, and they are fun and easy to make. Buy a real board or just tape some pieces of A4 or A3 together. Pick up some magazines. It does not have to be new magazines – you can get them from anywhere. Flick through the magazines and find pictures that make you feel good – ones that represent things that you want to experience. For example, if you want more laughter in your life then cut out pictures of friends having a convivial dinner.

Note that you do not have to be super-clear before you start cutting and pasting the images. This process will help you gain clarity.

I recommend that you avoid black-and-white pictures. For me they have a bad connotation, feeling more like something from the past rather than from my future. I prefer bright, joyful, full-colour pictures. They might be of the exterior of a house, or of part of the interior, showing what your home will look and feel like. They might represent your new job environment – a picture of someone doing a presentation and clearly feeling comfortable in that role (if that would be something that appealed to you), or of people shaking hands and doing deals, money flowing – just whatever you want! Pick up some magazines, ask your friends for their old ones and start flicking through those pages. Start cutting them out, and then one day – or even now – you will be ready to put them together in a collage. I also like to cut out empowering words and phrases, such as 'passion', 'money flowing in', 'change is the word', or 'now is the time'. You will find such headings in the magazines. They will jump out at you. There are some people who get really systematic and scientific about this, for example creating mini vision boards for each particular area of their lives. You could make one for the type of car you want to attract, another one for how love will be expressed in your life, one for friendships, and yet another for the perfect job. Since we are talking about jobs right now, please put together a collage that will reflect the job environment you are looking for. That will help you get clearer and shift your energy. I promise that you will start feeling good. If you want to see samples of vision boards visit http://www.CoCreatingOurReality.com and type 'Vision Board' in the top right-hand corner of the website in the search box. You will find hundreds of examples of vision boards! They are so beautiful and inspiring! Check them out! I also recorded a how-to-create-vision-boards video a while back in Chicago. That video has received over 15,000 hits to date! See http://www.youtube.com/watch?v=Q-W8aKrHeWQ.

If you have kids, do it with them. They can also create their own, as Martta, a CCOR Co-Creator from Finland, says (see http://www. cocreatingourreality.com/profile/Martta). Her kids loved it, and their vision board included a collage showing them meeting Mickey Mouse in Eurodisney! How great!

Another thing about vision boards is that you can make them small enough to slip into your wallet or big enough to cover an entire wall in your home. They can be private or on public display. They can be beautiful and artistic. Just do it the way you want; it is a matter of what pleases you, what makes you feel good, and gives you the feeling now of how you will feel when you have that dream job. Obviously, you can do this even if you are currently employed but wish to attract a different atmosphere and better relations with your colleagues. If you have a difficult boss, for instance, and there are people in your workplace who rub you up the wrong way, then cut out some pictures of people getting along, ones that show smiles, friendly acknowledgements and agreements. Place them somewhere prominent and make a point of looking at them every day for a reasonable length of time.

Visualisation

Visualisation is another way to shift energy. Close your eyes and imagine yourself in your new situation. The vision board will help you conjure some images and be clear about what you want. We are not all natural dreamers, but this should make it possible for you. It will give you both the desire and the ability to dream, giving you 'permission' to do it, and so to start attracting that fabulous job!

THE IMPORTANCE OF NOT SIMPLY TOLERATING A MEDIOCRE JOB

Talking about dream jobs, I meet a lot of people who simply go to work mechanically, tolerating the fact that they are not happy in their positions. They think 'this is as good as it can get' or that they 'should be grateful for having a job in the first place'. I am blessed with being a passionate person and, generally, I have loved what I have done up to now. However, I know there is now a different direction for me to take. That was why I was fired. Feeling there was more for me, I was not performing to the best of my ability. There was always a conversation going on in my head, saying that there was something else. That I should feel good about what I did. I had many such pesky thoughts, and ultimately they led to me being fired. Looked at another way, my doubts caused others in the company to have doubts about me.

WE ARE BORN WITH EXTRAORDINARY POWERS!

That's the sort of thing that could easily happen to you too, in the present economic climate when businesses may be seeking to lay people off. Looked at in that way, you might as well attract the sort of job that you would be really passionate about, that you would love. Imagine going to work every day and just loving it! You spend a lot of time at work so it makes sense to make sure that it is something you enjoy. There is no point feeling bad, waking up in the morning feeling 'yucky', and groaning to yourself about another miserable day in the trenches. It's no fun feeling like that; this is not what you signed up for. I am telling you now that it is not supposed to feel that way; it is supposed to feel good. So, if you start to notice that you are feeling resentful about your job, recognise that you need to shift your way of thinking and realise, 'Yes I can love my job and be fulfilled. This is possible!' This reminds me of my friend Hank in Michigan, who told me once: 'Lilou, life is too short. Start with the dessert!'

The vision board will really help that unfold, and visualisation will help you get clear and feel it and *know* it is possible. The subconscious does not make any distinction between what is real and what is not. When you visualise it – your dream job – your subconscious will think this is your reality, so you will attract more of those moments (people, conversations…) that will make it happen. You will feel lighter at work, or, if you are unemployed and looking for a job, then you will be more optimistic about the situation and more creative; you will open up and find the right information, looking in ways you wouldn't have if you had been stressed. You were born with incredible capabilities, with extraordinary powers. Why not use them?

PERMISSION TO FEEL GOOD IN 'BAD' CIRCUMSTANCES

I think many of us have the preconceived notion that we should not feel good when we lose our jobs. I found myself in a strange position, as I felt good about being fired, and so I started interrogating myself along these lines: 'What is wrong with me? This is not normal; I should feel sad, angry…'

Today, on my way to the gym, I was listening to some music on my iPod when the battery ran out. 'Oka-a-y,' I thought, 'What else can I do?' I took out my iPhone and looked through the songs on it and my eye alighted on the audio version of one of Jerry and Esther Hicks' latest books, *Money & the Law of Attraction, Learning to Attract Wealth, Health and Happiness*. So I picked a track of this at random, and, of course, it was the perfect track for me to listen to at that point. It was all about feeling good, and how you can tell if you are on the right path etc. Listening to this boosted my energy even more, as you can imagine. I felt increasingly joyous as it gave me the reassurance I needed that 'it is OK to feel good, it is OK'.

FACING REALITY

I am interrupting my steam-of-consciousness memos and reportage here to make an important point. I think it is better not to read, watch or listen too much to the mainstream media, such as the TV news, while you are searching for a job. To some extent, the news is only what the government wants to say and wants you to hear. You are better off finding blogs by independent journalists or passionate people from all over the world who want to share valuable information. The picture they present will most likely be quite negative right now, as we are seeing not only individual bankruptcies but also the collapse of companies. It is important to look squarely at this truth.

IT IS NOT ABOUT WISHFUL THINKING

The Law of Attraction is different from wishful thinking or positivity: you will be all the more powerful for facing the reality of things. If you are fearful about what is happening, it is not the news doing it to you; it is your own fearfulness that is the problem and this is what you need to confront. I repeat: this experience can only strengthen you. There is nothing more powerful than creating a new life for yourself from a place of total awareness and consciousness. I would, however, recommend that you surround yourself with positive people. Go and get some!

THE IMPORTANCE OF HAVING SOMEONE WITH WHOM TO SHARE YOUR DREAMS

I am going to call Cilou (that's the nickname of my friend Cécile Madelenat)… (Yes, I know: Cilou and Lilou! Actually, we would joke about this as it felt a bit like 'dumb and dumber'.) Cécile now lives in the Champagne region of France although I met her in Miami several years ago. She is a phenomenal person. I miss her. Anyway, I am going to call her now as I told her I had lost my job and she said she was available to speak about it. She said she was there for me, but I do

/lights'

not want to 'cry on her shoulder'. I do not want to indulge too much in negative feelings. Instead I will be sharing with her what positive things are coming out of the loss of my job, and I feel good about sharing the idea of the book with her. She is one of those people with whom I can share my dreams. She always fights my corner. (I think that it is important for you too – to find someone with whom you can share your dreams – someone who is close to you, but who is not going to judge you, no matter how crazy and wild those dreams might be.) So I will be able to share that with her, and we are going to have a great and inspiring conversation that will, I hope, open up even more things. Sorry, no: '...that *definitely* will open up more things!'

THE IMPORTANCE OF KEEPING A JOURNAL

I have been keeping a diary noting every single step along the way; from the moment I lost my job. I encourage you also to list every little thing that happens, either as it occurs, or at the end of each day. I do it moment by moment as things unfold, because I want, very strongly, to have something happen, and to happen quickly. The more I am in the flow, the more I feel good, and the quicker I believe things will manifest. I am very much 'full-on' in this regard, determined to demonstrate the power of the Law of Attraction to you.

THE BIG 'COMING OUT': PUBLICLY ANNOUNCING THE LOSS OF MY JOB

Today, on Day 35, Season 11 of the '100-Day Reality Challenge', I'll be making a video announcing that I have lost my job (later posted here: http://www.cocreatingourreality.com/video/day-35-i-lost-my-job) It is a pretty big deal for me to broadcast this to the world, particularly considering that at work my boss did not put it in such a way that people would necessarily have realised that I was being fired. He announced it very professionally, saying something like I was moving to something new... 'moving to pastures new', I think he said. ('Yes, actually, the grass

41

is greener here, Peter!') It was pretty funny that he used that turn of phrase. He must have known that I was going to start something new for myself, and not go back to Internet marketing. It was nice of him to do that, but now I am announcing it to everyone: I am 'coming out'!

I am putting myself out there because I know there are many people who will give me support, and, more importantly, because I believe I may help to empower people – those who have lost their jobs too, and those who are simply unhappy in their work. (You can access all the videos I have made since the loss of my job on my YouTube channel www.youtube.com/liloumace. Click on the playlist called 'From job loss to dream job'.)

BEING UNCONVENTIONAL

I am going to document this journey on video. I want it to be very juicy, very informative. I won't tell viewers all the details of my project – the type of book I am putting together – but I will share the journey, and hopefully the videos I make now and subsequently will be viewed by millions, and all these people will be supportive of the book, which will demonstrate a new way of thinking, a new way of viewing things. By finding your own way of approaching problems, and really tuning in, by doing what feels good, you will, ultimately, make discoveries and create some great and unique things.

This is why I think it is also important for me not to present the ideas themselves in a conventional way, the way other people do it. I declare today that this book will be unique in the way it is written, put together, published and marketed. It will be one of the best selling books ever. That is what I declare right now at this stage, when I have barely recorded 40 little memos and I have no idea how it is going to turn out. …On second thoughts, I *do* know how it is going to turn out. I know it may seem pretty bold to say that, but this is how the Law of Attraction works – certainty goes a long way! Knowing

JOB SEARCHES ON GOOGLE: AN EPIDEMIC!

I am amazed how all this is unfolding. One of the things I look at, as part of Internet marketing, is keywords, to see how many people are searching for what. Obviously, it was important for me to find out what was happening with regard to keywords related to searching for a job, given the topic of this book; and I am astounded by the figures I found.

I just did a video on job-search keywords, in which I presented some of the interesting data I have found. If searching for jobs were a disease you could say there's an online epidemic right now – *that* many people are looking!

An Internet marketer for the last eight years, I found it particularly instructive to look at the monthly job-search figures in Google. The number of people searching for the term 'job loss' in January was 40,500, double the average of 22,200 for previous months, and there's a high demand for entry-level jobs. For example, search terms related to temporary, entry-level PA positions in Google and PA jobs showed a 45 % increase in January 2009 over the usual monthly figure, so those are big numbers we're talking about. This high demand for entry-level jobs was reflected in the healthcare and banking/finance sectors, and looking specifically at what fields of employment are up in terms of job-related searches, in this last category they have gone from an average of a million per month to 1.5 million. People also seem to be looking for more secure employment, such as government jobs, the interest in which appears to have increased dramatically. Another revelation was that many people appear keen to sharpen their skills in areas like interview techniques and job-application procedures. Finally, I suspect that people are more technical in what they're doing: they using the Internet more and in more sophisticated ways.

In summary, then, there are big jumps pretty much across the board. People are really searching this time, and those numbers are scary, so I'm pleased that I posted a video on it on YouTube: http://www.youtube.com/watch?v=1e47ye0H2xM. I am so hopeful that it will be of great interest to people; I certainly find the data interesting! In fact, it was a real eye-opener for me. I had not realised how bad it was.

HELPING OTHERS AND HELPING MYSELF

I'm a YouTube partner, so that means that the more people who click on the advertisements adjacent to my videos, the more money I make. I probably make about $300 to 500 a month at the moment, and have about 3,000 to 5,000 video-views a day, and those numbers are increasing all the time. Theoretically, they should be significantly boosted when I touch on a 'bigger' topic (a more searched one), and I am doing that through this process of exploring my desire to write a book on the application of the Law of Attraction to job-hunting. I am sharing my journey as it unfolds, which is making me feel pretty exposed and vulnerable, but this is bound to make it more helpful to others and, therefore, as my goal is to help others (especially in light of the current situation), I am sure it's the right thing to do. I feel I'm on the right path here: it should help many people and earn me some money, and the two are inseparable.

I think it's empowering to see the flow of things in this way. My idea is to keep up this comprehensive diary of the various things that are happening and to incorporate a sort of 'feel-good gratitude journal', and I encourage you to do this too, at least on a daily basis, keeping up to speed with what you're doing. I'm also going to continue with my videos, because I find these very empowering and they will also help other people along the way. So I'm committed to both, and that's it for now…

AN OBSERVATION ON OBSERVATION

I don't think I'm going to sleep tonight; I'm so pumped up. Sometimes we fail to see things because our minds are not open. Things can be there, right in front of us, but because we think they do not exist, or because we think they're not there or they're just not for us, or are opportunities that are beyond our capabilities to take advantage of, we just don't see them. Actually, things show up in life according to what we think – and what we think is possible – so if you're convinced there's no spinach in your fridge then you probably won't see the spinach that is there. (Yes, I just spent five minutes looking in my fridge!)

Look up

There's this video on YouTube (http://www.youtube.com/user/thinkofanelephant) where this Australian guy, Paul Bailey, just asks you to look around the room you're in... Why don't we do the exercise right now? Assuming you're in a room somewhere, think of a colour. All right? Now, you're going to look around you for all the objects of that colour, OK? And then close your eyes and remember every one of those objects. When I did this exercise, it was almost as if I were blind. I chose purple, but, somehow, I was just not looking for purple things; I could see plenty of yellow things, but purple things were, indeed, there. You really have to look, and have an open mind!

CREATING CONTEXT: 'IN THE QUESTIONING OF THINGS'

That exercise demonstrates the importance of what I call 'creating context'. When you're open to something, or simply asking for advice, the answer will come. I ask for higher guidance or for signs. I ask for answers to my questions. That sort of approach puts you 'in the questioning of things'. It's the opposite of shutting things down by saying, 'Oh, that's just not possible.' Believe me, what you might have thought 'not possible' is exactly what will show up if you keep an open mind. Keep this in mind when searching for a job – for your dream job: stay 'in the questioning'.

To illustrate the point I have just made, I had no idea that I was going to write a book. The starting point, some time ago, was when I announced, 'I'm looking for higher guidance', with no clear end in mind. I know that I love TV, networking, creative events, sharing, empowering millions of people, etc., but as for finding a job, I just didn't know how that was going to happen. Things just unfolded. At the time of writing this I am thinking that the book might be called *Diary of a Job Seeker* or *Diary of a Dream Job Seeker*.

I just had a phenomenal conversation with one of my friends, Chantal. We talked of various things that had been happening in our lives, and, of course, I updated her on my situation. The conversation confirmed the merits of the diary idea, and the thoughts that emerged from it I record here.

THE BOOK CONCEPT EMERGES

Unlike other 'diary books'

I am clear that it will not be anything like Bridget Jones's diary. Neither, obviously, will it in any way resemble the famous diary of Anne Frank. The publication of Lilou's diary, however, will be an historical event at an historical moment, because its purpose will be to help people get through the storm of job losses at this time of financial crisis. This book will cross genres, being as much a journal as an exercise book, and it will also contain narrative and biography, a diary of daily life but with theory and practical exercises. It'll be an all-in-one. It'll be easy to read. It'll be low-budget. It'll be straightforward and fun. It'll make a great gift. It'll surely be a no-brainer for people to buy it, for perhaps £10 maximum, but a single-digit number would be better.

Enjoyment, reality, awakening consciousness and appealing to all

The idea would then be to do a series of similar books and seek to recreate the enjoyment that people had when they were children, reading their way through the books of their favourite authors. The series will start, then, with a little story of someone who is finding the job of her dreams and it will be inspirational, invigorating… It'll bring people back to their own reality and make them ask themselves the right questions. It'll be for unemployed people looking for work, and for those unhappy with their current positions. This book, therefore, should appeal to a huge number of people – practically everybody. The time is certainly right. There are many people currently out of work. I sense that many of them do not know what to do in life, although they do know that they don't want to go back to their old reality. They believe that they deserve better, and they want something that they're happy with, so there's an opportunity for an awakening of consciousness here. This book will certainly be consciousness-awakening, so I am confident of its success. Some videos on YouTube have already started showing how important the subject is right now, and how many people relate to it, so it makes sense not to deal specifically with the Law of Attraction, in isolation, and thereby only attract people who want to hear about that; it's a question of attracting people who want to find the job of their dreams (or just simply find a job) and, as I've said, that applies to most of us, so Insha'Allah

OPENING TO REALITY AND OTHER INPUTS

So that was my conversation with Chantal, a really good conversation that opened up and clarified a lot of my ideas regarding the book She's very knowledgeable and she plugged in some pieces that had been missing, and I realised that I have to see the reality. Looking at the figures, and seeing just how many people are seeking jobs, really woke me up to just how dramatic the situation is. I came to understand that previously I had only been looking only at positive news – or avoiding the news altogether – so I'd effectively been out of the world. I think it's important now to open up and really see what's going on.

Chantal recommended 'Blog of The Apocalypse' by Pierre Jovanovic, and the blog of a Telegraph journalist, Richard Evans. Both are apparently phenomenal, so I'm going to look at them and step back a bit from things, and allow myself a bit of space so that I can create new things – new models, and new ways of thinking.

It's about being receptive and sharing… If we're going to improve things then, to some extent, it must be about us opening up, both within ourselves and to others, and sharing things and helping each other.

SLIGHT DOUBTS, AND BACK ON TRACK

Shortly after my conversation with Chantal, negative thoughts started popping into my head, such as, 'Oh, I have to be real too… I want to write a book and live my dream, but am I going to be able to financially sustain myself…?' This is probably typical of the kind of interior conversation we experience when we're seeking a job. I cannot allow those fears to hold me back this time. As Jack Canfield says, F.E.A.R. means False Evidence Appearing Real.

I must remind myself why I'm doing this, what the fundamental aim is. I have to keep the focus on attracting my dream job. For some people, it might be starting their own business or it might be writing a book etc., but even once one broad avenue has been chosen there are various possible solutions, and by staying open they are more likely to occur to you. In fact, the conversation helped me see that if your aim is to write a book there are two major routes to follow (strictly speaking, there are more than two options): either you self-publish or you find a publisher. My ultimate aim, whichever route I go down, is to empower millions. One of the first possibilities to present itself is for the book to sell in large volumes, but along the way I shall need to find the funds to support my writing and to make the book available to a wide audience. Then, certainly, other ventures could potentially open themselves up. But I feel the book should be first.

A BOOK PROPOSAL

I think it makes sense to start with a book proposal – a document outlining the nature of the book – and so I've decided to write one. Stephanie, in New York City, could help me do this, but she would charge me quite a lot of money. I don't feel it is appropriate or necessary to spend this right now, so I am thinking of writing the proposal myself and then having her review it, and possibly helping edit the book itself.

LISTEN TO YOUR INNER VOICE

It's important to listen to our inner voice, the little voice of our heart that tells us that something else is possible. We often overlook it because of the loud chatter going on in our heads. I think we're now in a situation where we really need to listen to our hearts rather than just think, think, think. My dad calls it the intelligence of the heart. I call it a message from the soul. Sandy Grason calls it our inner voice.

When I was at the gym this morning and experienced this moment when ideas were starting to flow, I felt this deep inner knowing that I'm meant to write this book right now, and this knowing was expressed in a very low voice. I had often heard about it from other people, but experiencing it for myself was really something, and now that I have I can describe it properly to you. It's a very peaceful, grounding and nurturing voice – sort of a mothering voice – that just tells you, 'This is what you're supposed to do, this is it...' and it's very reassuring.

It's not at all frightening, despite the considerable power of it – you certainly sense the impact it can have. Listen to your inner voice, and you'll never go wrong!

THE PURPOSE OF THIS BOOK

This memo forms the introduction to this book, so go back and read it again, and you will now understand where it fitted into my train of thought!

WHERE IS GARY?

I just sent an email to Gary, with whom I recorded a few visualisation and meditation tracks for a CD, back in November in Florida. Unfortunately, Gary never sent them to me, despite me asking and asking, but I guess it wasn't meant to be at that time. That was one of those doors that were closed and which I tried to force from time to time, to no avail. Well, I just sent him a message via Facebook, but instead of just asking him for the CD again, I asked for help, and he must then have realised the situation.

I felt like I had been begging him to send the CD material to me over the past few months. We're now in February and my initial idea had been to launch he CD at the beginning of January. So, hopefully, we can do this now, and it should certainly have the potential to create… Not 'hopefully'! I cancel that thought. No, this is the perfect time to launch it, and it was not supposed to be launched any earlier. This is going to help me sell a lot of my meditation stuff, and create a source of revenue that will support me. This is the context I now choose!

Actually, looking back, I was probably not ready a couple of months ago, because I didn't have the time and so I probably wouldn't have launched it properly – powerfully – putting in the energy that I needed to put in to make it successful. Right now, by contrast, I'm at a place where I have that time and the product is ready, and Gary can put in even more energy, as (I'm sure) he wants to support me in what's happening in my life in general. I'm very confident about how things are going to unfold from here.

THE SYNERGY OF THE BOOK AND CD

I'm also very grateful because the book is not ready right now but the CD is, so that will be two things coming out, and the one will surely help the other. They could even come out at the same time, although I don't know how long the whole process will take for the book. I don't think it will take that long to get the CD finished, as the tracks are ready, so it's just a matter of creating the cover and finding the title, and doing this and that, which I can do right now, and that's about it.

SEEKING SUPPORT, PRACTICAL HELP AND DIVINE GUIDANCE

This will be an opportunity for me to find the support that I need from friends and talented people I know, people who can help me put this CD out. I'm thinking especially of the cover of the CD, for which I might possibly seek help from Marc Holland here in the UK, who works for the company I was working for. I really love what he does, and he'd probably create an amazing cover. Marc is definitely a genius of a creative director!

That's all for today. It's midnight. Before going to bed, though, I'm going to do a quick reiki session, and also ask for higher guidance during my sleep: ask to be divinely guided and to have some new ideas so that I wake up recharged. I want to have a good night's sleep tonight and wake up fully alive. Bye.

THE BENEFIT OF BEING OPEN ABOUT LOSING MY JOB

I think the fact that I'm really out in the open again now, vulnerable and exposed, can only add to the power of my story to inspire. I would like to think that by opening myself up to the world I am proving just how powerful the Law-of-Attraction tool can be in our lives! I didn't have to share the fact that I was being made 'redundant', but I chose to do so on Facebook, on YouTube, and in other ways, making sure that everybody heard about it, even the people inside my company. I am fully ready to 'release' and 'be with it', and have set the scene for sharing my journey, a journey that I am certain will make a difference to other people's lives as I demonstrate the tools I use to realise my dreams.

I declare that when the book comes out, it will be a smash hit. Yeah, baby!

YOUR HEART'S DESIRES: SHIFTING MY MOOD

Today is Thursday, and I woke up a little bit negative – just not quite as pumped up as yesterday – so I did a meditation, one of the ones I've recorded. It's out there for free on the net. It's called *Effective Meditation | Manifest what you really Want NOW!* but I should perhaps have labelled it *Your Heart's Desires (video link http://www. youtube.com/watch?v=RQLXTF7FT_c)*. As you might expect, it's about visualising what you truly want, bringing it out from the depths of your being, and fully feeling it. It also has various exercises concerning your heart and your true desires etc. In summary, it's a good little ten-minute visualisation that helps shift your mood and set the tone for your day. Anyway, I have just done it and now I'm feeling empowered to start typing up what I recorded yesterday, and take things from there.

I must admit, though, that I have been hesitating about going to the gym. Knowing, however, how much the ideas were flowing there yesterday, and how good it felt, I will 'get my ass in gear' and give myself a bit of a nudge!

THE WONDERS OF TECHNOLOGY

It's now 9.30 a.m. I'm constantly amazed by the power of technology, and I'm so thankful for 'Retro 9', the recording device I'm currently using on my iPhone. Now I have just downloaded yet another little gadget, or software 'widget'. In the past I have downloaded and learnt to use various such devices, and they've enabled me to 'write' this book – or to speak out this book, if you will. This latest one adds even more to my iPhone's capabilities. It allows me to upload any recordings I make to an IP address, which should then be accessible to anyone I choose, anywhere in the world. This should certainly help when it comes to transcription! Also, I currently have an 8 GB iPhone, but I believe that I could record up 290 hours on the 16, if I wanted to get one. Amazing, indeed!

SEEKING A TRANSCRIPTION TYPIST

You may guess from the foregoing that typing all this in doesn't really feel too good; I feel that by transcribing my recordings myself I might be taking too much on. I am considering hiring someone help, perhaps somebody who is currently out of work and is at home searching for a job, someone ready to do this at a great rate per hour and who will have the time and motivation to do it well. My intention today is to attract someone suitable, who could start typing up my recordings pretty much immediately. I'll need somebody who's technically savvy, to some extent, and someone who is trustworthy, can work quickly and is happy to contribute. Such a person would be perfect!

Back to the subject of being 'pumped up'… You can see how ideas and events are continuing to occur – to flow – thick and fast. Just listening to that visualisation recording got me 'back into the mojo'. I'm very much empowered again.

SUPPORT FROM THE '100-DAY REALITY CHALLENGE' COMMUNITY

I feel so blessed. I just posted my Day 35 video yesterday (*I've Lost My Job*), and now I'm looking at the comments that have been posted (http://www.cocreatingourreality.com/video/day-35-i-lost-my-job). I've received the most amazing messages of support.

One of them comes from CCOR member Eric – dear Eric – who, at the end of his pretty long comments, writes:

> *Dear Universe*
> *Lilou is such a blessing in my life. I can hardly describe*
> *what her positive existence means to me. Dear Universe,*
> *I intend for Lilou exactly what she desires. Please provide*
> *this sweet soul with the sustinence we all need. Dear*
> *Universe, wrap your arms around this wonderful woman*
> *and cherish her as I do. She is a leader, a warrior, a*
> *philosopher, a friend to all of us. Dear God, please reward*
> *Lilou for paying it forward at every turn! Selfless, to a*
> *large degree. Giving, always! Please hear my calls for*
> *action -- I guess I have not asked for anything as much.*

As I say, this was from Eric, one of the co-creator members (Eric's profile page: http://www.cocreatingourreality.com/profile/Eric) and I'm in tears and I feel so blessed right now, and so grateful for having this community which I co-founded back in 2005. My life would certainly not be what it is, were it not for CCOR and all the people who continue to join (it's free!) and participate in the '100-Day Reality

Challenge' and who send me emails and messages every day (both through the CCOR website and YouTube). The energy I put in I get back tenfold. Truly, I wouldn't be where I am today without every single member of this mutually supportive community. It's an amazing, divine phenomenon that seems to provide support at those crucial times when we (any of us associated with the community) go through tough patches.

THE IMPORTANCE OF BEING PART OF A COMMUNITY

I think it's important for all of us, as human beings, to belong to such a community, where we can really engage with others. I based this cyberspace community on the Law of Attraction, but there many other communities out there, for example for cat lovers or for those wanting to write a book – great places to find advice and encouragement. One of the things I particularly appreciate about the CCOR community is that you can use it to help yourself achieve just about anything you want to do. There are, for example people using the '100-Day Reality Challenge' (details on www.CoCreatingOurReality.com) to help them lose weight or attract more money, an d to date over 170 sub-groups have been created. The '100-Day Reality Challenge' is very simple. Participants simply set themselves various goals for each 100-day period, and then, through blogs and videos, share their unfolding journeys with each other, offering each other help and encouragement along the way. Wonderful friendships have developed and, speaking for myself, the nurturing, uplifting messages I receive, such as Eric's, really touch me. Here's another example:

> *I am so excited for you!! I don't want to jump into your business…*
> *But… just wanted to say Jump! Fly! Soar! You can do anything*
> *that you want right now!!! I can totally see you coaching… I see*
> *you inspiring people and starting today making money without a*
> *"job"!! :) I see so much GREATNESS Ms. Lilou!!*

That was from Alexandra Jaye, another member of the '100-day Reality Challenge' community (www.cocreatingourreality.com/profile/AlexandraJaye). Another person, WealthyApple (http://www.cocreatingourreality.com/profile/wealthyapple) says:

Thank you for your honesty and truth. You are certainly aligned to go on and do amazing things. You're a true inspiration!

And this is right now nourishing my soul, let me tell you! Another one, from Beth, says:

I got goose bumps listening to you – the good kind of goose bumps lol I feel so much energy coming through you – it's wonderful! Cannot wait to hear tomorrow's update :)

I am sure you can imagine how fulfilling it is to read such messages, and how it's filling my tank of inspiration right now!

Here's an extract from a comment by Anne, still on the same video:

What a wonderful, energetic video! You are one courageous woman. I just can feel you're going to manifest something awesome with this kind of energy. Good luck in all your ventures.

And then Eric again (the first part is truly inspiring):

Lilou, this is one of the most honest vids I've seen in a long time. Talk about pride! You and I talked about the recession, it sucks! I just cannot picture a world without Lilou blossoming. I have not read the feedback from your vid yet. I am sure it is plentiful, but I want you to know from me that you are loved across the world and that you can achieve anything you desire. I really believe that, even if you don't. You said there have been signs, and I think they are short-sighted to let you go, but I'm sure all CCOR folks will rally at your attitude.

Another comment to this video, this time from Mascha (http://www.cocreatingourreality.com/profile/Mascha):

OMG Lilou!!! I sooo love you!! Turning this situation into a positive, juice one is very powerrrrful!!! Having time to follow your intuition and inspired actions towards raw food & wellness. Higher guidance is with you, you're so blessed!! The answers will come to you... just listen. Your talents are calling you~*YEAH TO FEELING GOOD!!!

Audrey (http://www.cocreatingourreality.com/profile/AUDREY) comments:

Good for you Lilou. It's amazing how you can save money in other areas so you can enjoy the luxuries you deserve.

Rachel (http://www.cocreatingourreality.com/profile/RachelGalvin) says:

Sounds like when I quit my job at the magazine! I loved your raw food interview, by the way. Maybe you should write a raw food book! What about doing your TV show there?

Well, good idea, Rachel! It will certainly be one of the things I'll be up to in the near future. Just stay tuned in, my dear Rachel.

The latest comment – one of the latest comments – comes from LizBeth (http://www.cocreatingourreality.com/profile/ElizabethHillery):

Dear Lilou: You are more "clear" than you have been in 6 months. By that I mean there was something different about you since you took this job in England. I can't describe it really ... sort of pall around you no matter what else you were talking about. You now have the vibrancy back.

Yes, Elizabeth. I do feel I have the vibrancy back, and I'm definitely going to move forward and continue along this way because I feel alive again since I was lost my job, and I don't want to let my fear stop me from living this dream.

TIME TO LIVE OUR DREAMS!

It is now time to live our dreams. My dream is to have a TV show and empower millions of people daily but, you know, it could be an Internet TV show. It could be a book, or seminars. All those are things that could happen, and now it's time! Now, it's time to make them happen, and have the money flowing in, and access this extraordinary power that we all have, that we have been given; when you begin practising it you'll see that the Law of Attraction is truly astounding! I challenge you to start by attracting a parking spot, for example, or the arrival of a bus just as you walk up to a bus stop. I think you'll be amazed. It'll start building up then, as your confidence grows, and, before you know it, you'll be off and away, attracting bigger and bigger things at will!

HOW I MET OPRAH WINFREY: THE POWER OF DECLARATIONS.

I'm in Season 11 of the '100-Day Reality Challenge' now, which means I've been consciously working for over a thousand days on implementing the Law of Attraction, declaring the things that I want, and practising methodically while I broadcast my progress on the Internet by video and on blogs. One of my favourite stories (and the most viewed on YouTube) is the one about how I met Oprah Winfrey. Tears come to my eyes thinking about stories like this, and of how blessed I was in Season 4 of the '100-Day Reality Challenge'.

I moved to Chicago after living in Miami for six years. About a month after I arrived I met Bryan, dear Bryan. He invited me for dinner at *Marché* in the West Loop of Chicago, and as we were having dinner in this beautiful French restaurant, I found myself telling him how much I admired Oprah Winfrey, for herself as a person and for what she's done in the world. What a great woman! – definitely one of my role models. To my surprise and delight, Bryan said, 'Well, we're right around the corner from Harpo Studios. Why don't we drop by?'

Indeed, only three blocks along, was the Harpo Studios building, with 'The Oprah Winfrey Show' emblazoned on it. My heart was pounding. A little girl who'd just been told she was going to Disneyland could scarcely have been so excited. Well, at that point I simply got my picture taken and then, *voilà*, I went back home and the next morning did a video blog to update people around the world on how I was doing on my '100-day Reality Challenge'. This video is still on YouTube, by the way, 25,000 video views later, (http://www.youtube.com/watch?v=qlmTM4rtyv8) and I know it has inspired people to do what I did... Exactly what did I do? I declared on the video: 'I want to meet Oprah Winfrey before the end of the year. I want to be in the audience of *The Oprah Winfrey Show*.'

That was in November 2006. Two days later – no joke – two days later, Bryan, with whom I had had dinner, bumped into Oprah Winfrey herself in the elevator of the Ritz Carlton in Chicago. He barely recognised her. She had no makeup on, and was standing there in sweatpants with her bodyguard. Bryan was a bit shocked, meeting her like that, although I don't think he realised at the time that it was no coincidence but a demonstration of the Law of Attraction. I think he understands this now! Don't you, Bryan? Anyway, he gathered his wits and found himself saying to The Big O: 'I just met Lilou. She's just arrived from Miami, and one of her dreams...' – he used the word 'dreams', a word Oprah loves – ' ... is to meet you, and be in the audience of your show.'

Generous as she is, Oprah then and there wrote a number down for him and said, 'Call this person and you'll have two tickets for tomorrow's show. Just be sure to be there by noon.' Wow!

Bryan called me right after this happened and I started shaking. Even I, familiar with the power of the Law of Attraction, couldn't believe what had happened. 'Wowwwwwwwwwwwwww!' I blurted, 'This is happening really fast. Is that for real?' I couldn't let myself believe it, because it was just so good! I said, 'I'll only believe it when I see it.'

The next day there we were, in front of Harpo Studios, and we called to one of Oprah's assistants through a back door. She said, 'I cannot believe Oprah did this. She usually doesn't do things like this at the last minute. She went to check with Oprah herself, and came back five minutes later. Within minutes we were in the audience of *The Oprah Winfrey Show.* Magical!

DREAM JOBS – MORE THAN COINCIDENCE!

And guess what? The show was about dream jobs! So again no coincidence there! This was a sign, as my dad would say. In the course of the show Oprah described what a phenomenal career she has had, about how busy she is in her daily life and about how blessed she felt etc., and then a couple of other people described their dream jobs. Throughout it all I sat basking in such a feeling of gratitude that I couldn't speak. I just listened and soaked it all up, struggling to come to terms with the fact that I had this famous Oprah Winfrey right there, only a couple of metres below and in front of me, and she had invited us to be there! And it wasn't just the main show I would see that evening! I stayed for the Oprah after-show being recorded for the Oxygen channel. (I now know just how lucky I was, because since then I've been to the main show four times and I know that this doesn't happen every time.) During the after-show, Oprah asked, 'So where is Bryan? Bryan that I met last night?'

'Yeah, Oprah, I'm here.' Bryan stood up, and the microphone and cameras were on him.

Oprah continued, 'Well, yes, I was visiting Barbara Streisand, and then I met you and you told me your friend really wanted to meet me. Is this your friend?' She was looking at me.

So there I was – little Lilou, really, really shy – standing in front of the Big O, a smile of gratitude stretched ear to ear across my face. 'Hello, Mrs. Oprah,' I said, 'Yes, thank you for inviting us.' Overwhelmed, that was pretty much all I could get out. I was so grateful for what was happening. Exchanging even just a couple of sentences with her was a wonderful experience, but more was to come, because Oprah then invited us backstage. The official photographer took a picture of us with her and we had an opportunity to chat a bit more. Later we were sent the official picture – the one-and-only picture, because you are not allowed to take cameras to the Oprah show. To have that picture was just such a blessing, and a lovely permanent reminder of what's possible. Here is the video Bryan and I took outside Harpo Studios: http://www.youtube.com/watch?v=LMZfUHUnIXE (24,000 views to date).

INSPIRED BY OPRAH, I STARTED MY OWN TV SHOW!

The next day, I felt so motivated to get my own TV show off the ground. I thought to myself, 'Oh my God, Oprah's living her dream, and she made it happen. I can and should so the same. I will!' By then I had had my own Internet marketing company for some time, having started an Internet business back in 2001, not long after September 11. Initially it was an email company, then it became a website design and Internet marketing company. I wasn't doing too badly, on the whole, but there were rough patches, and I constantly had to chase clients and was just not 100% fulfilled. I was making a living, learning a lot, and enjoying the work most of the time, so I stuck at it, even if at times I felt my youth was passing me by. Most importantly, when I met Oprah, however, I realised that I had been hiding behind a computer screen. That I had said I wanted to empower people, but in reality I was cowering behind a screen instead of being in front of people and cameras. Anyway, when I saw Oprah talking about realising her dream job it was as if a big light went on: I would start my own show!

I searched online, trying to find out how to do it. Perhaps I should take a class, I thought: maybe I could find a free class at a university to learn how to become a journalist or TV presenter? I was really fired up, feeling great about it, and going with the flow. I made another declaration to the Universe, and after about two hours of fruitless research, I finally ran across CAN TV in Chicago. (One of the great things about the USA is that you can have your own cable TV show for practically nothing. I'm not sure if this exists in London or elsewhere in the UK.) The purpose of this particular channel was to give Chicagoans a voice, a forum to express their opinions. Generally speaking, as long as the quality of the show is satisfactory (which applies to most of the material submitted) they accept it for broadcast. There are, of course, some rules – you have to register as a producer, for example – but the cost of it all is pretty marginal, such that practically anyone can access it. You won't be surprised to learn that I immediately contacted CAN TV to find outmore. (A video blog on this may be viewed at: http://www.youtube.com/watch?v=gYN9HhNtz0A.) I was thrilled with the whole idea but knew nothing about how it worked. I went along to an introductory session and they told me things like: 'You can get up to a million viewers!'

Wow! I was sure I was on track!

JUICY LIFE

The very next day a producers' class was due to start, so I signed up. Once trained, I had to start thinking of the concept for a show and manifesting people to join the team I would need – a volunteer team to record and edit etc. – so I posted some ads on CAN TV, and before long I was creating a TV show called *Live a Juicy Life*.

Well, the programme was originally titled *My Juicy Life*. I wanted to update people on a day-to-day basis, to make it a sort of reality show on my meetings with interesting people, the main idea being to interview the authors of self-development books (an avenue I have continued to follow). I decided to rename it *Live a Juicy Life* to make it clear that the show was not only going to be about *my* juicy life. The original title, however, had been conceived with the thought that people would feel a sense of ownership of the show, and, more subtly, a sense of stewardship of their own lives, by virtue of the title: 'Oh, *My Juicy Life*. Have you seen *My Juicy Life*?' In other words, they would start to admit to themselves that they had (potentially) a juicy life. It's self-fulfilling when you start saying things like, 'Yes, I have a juicy life. Yes, I have an extraordinary life.' You begin to feel grateful for and alive to the good things in your life, and so you start attracting more of them! I use 'juicy', by the way, to mean passion and purpose – like when you squeeze an orange and you have all the juice and good stuff coming out of it. Anyway, it worked for me, as I had the opportunity to interview some wonderful people as part of the *Juicy Life* experience.

WHERE BIG INTENTIONS CAN TAKE YOU

Sandy Grason was my first guest on the show. Sandy and I co-founded the '100-Day Reality Challenge'. During this interview we discussed her book *Journalution: Journaling to Awaken Your Inner*

Voice, Heal Your Life and Manifest Your Dreams. She was an amazing guest who got me off to a flying start. (See http://www.SandyGrason.com)

Thereafter I continued to have a wonderful time, hosting and producing *Live a Juicy Life* and meeting many extraordinary people. I spoke to Karyn Calabrese about raw foods. I was able to interview John Gray, the author of *Men Are From Mars and Women Are From Venus*, and Sarah Caldicott, a great grandniece of Thomas Edison who co-authored a book on innovation based on Edison's principles. Judith Wright, the author of *The One Decision*, a phenomenal person whom I had met back in Miami, also made a very welcome appearance on the show.

Another notable interviewee was Kevin Ross, author of *Living the Designer Life*. My interview with Kevin took place on the same day as *The Oprah Winfrey Show* debut of *The Secret*, so you won't be surprised to learn that we intended to attract another ticket, and, yes, we were there in the audience! Jack Canfield, Rhonda Byrne, and other contributors to *The Secret* were guests, and it was great to be there. I want to thank you again, Oprah, for that. It was because I met you that not only that night, but much of my ongoing adventure was possible, and I was able to go on to live my dreams!

Speaking of thanks, I will be eternally thankful to Terry, John Beck and Elena Katardjieva who filmed and edited my show. Guys, you were fantastic! I want to acknowledge you for believing in me, and doing it all for nothing, even though you were not exactly wealthy. Together we made it possible. Thank you.

I should tell you a bit more about *Live a Juicy Life*. I did it on top of my day job (running my web agency), juggling the two over the entire course of the show. There were no advertisements and you could call it 'homemade', as it was filmed in my living room with the team of volunteers I have mentioned, using equipment borrowed from CAN TV. Nevertheless, we constantly improved as we went along, and the adventure was very fulfilling, as you will know by now! The initial struggle to get it off the ground, to attract an audience, and even to speak to the camera, were well worth it.

This whole episode is a perfect illustration of how the Law of Attraction works. Things start to manifest when you declare really big intentions. I declared that I wanted to empower millions of people, and then Sandy and Laura entered my life, which led to the '100-Day Reality Challenge' and my doing videos on YouTube. With that groundwork done, meeting Oprah and doing TV followed.

THE IMPORTANCE OF MOMENTUM

I allowed this all to happen, to unfold. You could say that I got out of the way of the ripple effect, and I let one thing lead to another. Another way of describing it would be to liken it to a snowball rolling down a hill. I didn't try to stop it; I stayed with it. When you're able to keep with it like that, it's amazing what happens.

To use yet another watery metaphor, at the outset you have to be able to catch the wave of an opportunity when it comes, so start paddling right now and start building movement and speed so when the wave arrives you can surf it and be off and away. If you're just sitting on your couch and doing nothing, then nothing's going to happen. You have to build momentum, and this doesn't mean just doing any old kind of action. No, it's about feeling good, so even if it's just going to the gym or walking in nature, or writing your journal (anything that you feel inspired to do), this is the kind of movement I'm talking about, that kind of positive movement. You must feel that you're moving forward and you're nourishing your body, and your mind/heart/soul... In summary: do things that feel good and that put you in a position to catch that wave when it comes.

TAKING STOCK: POTENTIAL SOURCES OF INCOME

I've just created a list of the various sources of revenue that I could be getting, if I am not to pursue an Internet marketing job but to focus on finding my dream job. One of these potential sources of revenue is the meditation CD.

Another possibility is the book idea. I'm thinking of calling it *Attracting Your Dream Job*. If I can get a publisher interested I might get an advance. I've heard, though, that it is quite difficult to get that kind of deal at the moment… No, I don't want to go down that route – that negative way of thinking – so I cancel that concern and I declare I will attract a publisher very quickly. One day I would love to be published by Hay House. This is Dr Wayne Dyer's publisher and it's owned by a wonderful woman called Louise Hay. Both of them have helped millions of people, and if we are where we are now, in terms of the evolution of our awareness as human beings, it is because of people like them, who are now in their early sixties and have stayed on track, sharing their hearts on the power of thoughts and intentions for decades. If I don't find a publisher, then I'll self-publish, but the way I feel at the moment I would rather find a publisher for the support this would provide.

Yet another source of revenue is my membership of the YouTube partner programme. As I explained before, the way this works is that the more people click on the advertisements next to my videos, the more money I make. You need to have many viewers and produce many videos to get a significant income from this, but since I'll be concentrating on making more of them, and on increasing subscribers, this should become meaningful. At the moment I'm earning about $300 a month this way. I'll do a bit of research on optimising things, as I believe that some YouTubers, such as Michael Buckley (http://www.youtube.com/user/WHATTHEBUCKSHOW), make over $100,000 a year through the partner programme, and Michael now has a contract with Fox.

I'm also intending to organise some singles' events. I organised one for Valentine's that had 600 RSVPs. I might even organise some paying ones, but I'm going to do a free one first, probably on March 3rd, and then… I could possibly do some seminars on the Law of Attraction, or on attracting your dream job. That could be either now or later on as part of the book promotion tour.

Speaking of the book again, I am also considering selling an audio version of it, which would be pretty much the same as the written version. I very much wanted to have the spoken memos that form the basis for most of this book put in a written format, but I think people might find it very inspiring to hear it all as well.

THOUGHTS OF A NEW COMPUTER

This all makes me think that I would like to update the Lilou Mace website (http://www.LilouMace.com) which leads to the thought that it would be a good idea to create a new website that would be easier to edit. Up until now I have been using iWork (one of the Mac tools) to create and update websites, but now that my original computer, which I used to set up my website, has broken down, I cannot update it from that, so I'm going to need to find another way…

I'm really tempted to get a new Apple computer right now, but I also have to balance priorities, and I do have a spare one that is still running. Whatever happens, I shall need to create a new website within the next three months. Hopefully, I'll be able to do it soon and have. Not 'hopefully' – cancel, cancel!

RESEARCHING BOOK IDEAS

My first and primary focus is the book proposal at this stage, and then getting a publisher, and so this is what I'm moving forward with. I'm browsing Amazon to see what is out there on the same topic. I found, for instance, *The 4-Hour Workweek: Escape 9-5, Live Anywhere and Join the New Rich* and *48 Hours to Doing What You Love*. There are many of them but really I'd like to something along the lines of *Bridget Jones's Diary* or *Anne Frank, The Diary of a Young Girl* but with a Jack Canfield-style title, something with a similar ring to his *Key to Living the Law of Attraction: A Simple Guide to Creating the Life of Your Dream*, but which will include my name so, for example, *Lilou: The Diary of a Dream Job Seeker* or *Lilou's Diary: Attracting a Dream Job/The Dream Job*. As you can see, the title is maturing and I'm letting it flow and asking for higher guidance.

WINE AND NETWORKING

Later on today, I have a fabulous Bordeaux tasting event that I will be attending, one that I have already paid for, thank God, because it's £30! I wouldn't have gone tonight if I hadn't already paid, but I'm definitely going to go and welcome the possibility of again meeting amazing people etc., etc., etc.

I'll continue my search – my progress – while I'm here in the kitchen. For some reason I'm more inspired every time I'm in this room, and even right now, although I'm not cooking, all of a sudden I have more ideas than when I'm in the living room or anywhere else. In any case, a change of scene is usually good…

NEW PERSPECTIVES

We don't all have the same approach to things, or receive the things that come to us in life the same way. I feel I am blessed because I love challenges and I love new things, but I realise that not everyone is comfortable with these. It doesn't necessarily make my life easy, or immediately perfect, but I accept this spirit of mine that thrives on change. Whatever our natures, however, we all are confronted by challenges, and fears that pop out in moments of insecurity. This is something I must keep in mind when writing the book – to try to be aware of everybody's perspective. I hope, as you read the book, you'll find something that will resonate with you, and also that you'll be able to relate to others' perspectives. In fact one of the aims of this book is to help you to follow this journey from my perspective – to lend you my eyes – partly in the hope that you might see your own situation from a different perspective, so that I can help you open up to some new ideas. I do hope you'll ride along with me, within this diary, this journal, and see how it unfolds, and that this will inspire you 'to jump on the wagon' at some point. You might just be inspired to take action in some way, and sometimes just one little thing – one little shift – can make a huge difference. By all means simply enjoy reading this, but keep an open mind to that possibility – you never know! And if it doesn't feel right at a certain point, just put the book down and then come back to it later. Don't force things; let them unfold.

A SONG?

This Katy Perry (http://www.katyperry.com/) pop song is going round and round in my head. I liked it. But instead of singing 'I kissed a girl and I liked it' I sing, 'I lost my job and I liked it. Na na na na.' I might want to rewrite the lyrics with that in mind. That would be fun.

THE IMPORTANCE OF DOING THINGS THAT MAKE YOU FEEL GOOD

I think the quicker you want to manifest your dream job, the more important it is to feel good, so the more you have to do stuff that feels great. It's a big challenge, a quantum leap of faith. Using the Law of Attraction to land a dream job requires boldness, and is a radically different approach from what we've been taught. *— Woman Lilou!*

I suggest you list ten things in your journal, right now, that you just love doing, that make you feel great, such as meeting a friend, having a bubble bath, getting a manicure done, a massage, going on a date, doing a seminar… whatever it is. Jot down ten things, the top ten things you enjoy (or you might want to write more and then narrow it down to ten, or even five) but write them down.

RECOGNISING INSPIRATIONAL THOUGHTS

You must do those things that will uplift and inspire you. Then you must follow where the resultant inspirational thoughts guide you. What do I mean by 'inspirational thoughts'? An inspirational – or inspiring – thought is one that draws you into doing something in an almost magnetic way; it calls you powerfully. We might not all have the same experience of these things, but I shall tell you how it works for me. I was, for example, very attracted to Jack Canfield's book just a couple of weeks ago. I wasn't sure exactly what the significance of this was at the time. There was something about it that I couldn't quite put my finger on, but I had the feeling that it was 'just right for me'. I looked at it again today, and the title jumped out – it really spoke to me, and gave me some major inspiration regarding the sort of title this book should have.

MAKE THE BOOK SUCCINCT?

Hey Stuart!! I miss you Stu! Yay!

I think I should keep this book succinct and straight to the point! I can see there's a risk of it becoming repetitive. There's a book I love called *The Little Money Bible: The 10 Laws of Abundance*. If you're looking for a book on attracting money and abundance in your life, I really recommend this one.   It's a short book – only so many pages, a quick read – and it stands on its own. It's just my favourite, a mine of good, condensed information. I can grab it, read it for a few minutes, and be empowered. I have highlighted some sections for quick reference. ...So I ask myself, why make my book long and thick when it's possible to have a short book that is truly inspirational? I think I'm going to go down that route, and create something short and sweet and powerful.

A SIGN?

A thing to remember is that you can't interpret everything that happens as a sign. The fundamental thing is to follow your heart. If you don't want to be overwhelmed by signs, but feel powerfully called to some of them while, for example, you're seeking a job or new solutions for some problem, then ask for higher guidance – ask for confirmatory signs that will truly show you what the next step should be, which could perhaps be as simple as making an enquiry. You don't have to have everything figured out. This process is not about figuring everything out in advance; rather it's about letting things unfold for you, and staying flexible.

FOLLOWING MY INTUITION LEADS TO FRESH INSPIRATION

I just felt the urge to stop at a gourmet pub around the corner. They've got fresh mint tea and simple nourishing food, and I have now ordered some. This place has a homey feel to it, and that's what

I want my book to have. So the branding of the book is actually quite homey, and down-to-earth, and the cover should convey the feeling that you're getting into somebody's intimate thoughts, somebody's secret garden, but it won't be ethereal, airy-fairy, at all: it will have a traditional and British flavour to it.

THIS BOOK IS NOT PRIMARILY ABOUT ITSELF!

At this point I should make sure that you understand that this narrative is not primarily about publishing a book, it's about following my journey (guided by the Law of Attraction), so I am simply relating what's happening for me. I want you, through this experience, to see what's fundamentally important, and interpret it in the light of what you yourself have always wanted to do, and perhaps you're not doing? Start allowing yourself to let those things develop. It's fascinating how it works.

Another thing I should re-state is that my intention is to attract my dream job. It might well be publishing this book and getting money from it – possibly selling it very rapidly to a publisher, perhaps in as little as two weeks. Yes, possibly I'll sign with a publisher and the money will flow in and this will be my dream job! There's nothing that I want more than to be able to travel to promote the book, to promote the ideas it contains, to continue to do the videos, and to be invited on TV to speak about the book, and right now I think everything is perfectly aligned to get that kind of exposure. Exposure is important to get the message across, and I feel as if Life is conspiring to help me. The Universe is on my side because I allow it to be, because I'm open to receiving higher guidance. I keep on asking for it, and I'm not being stopped by apparent setbacks. I'm continually progressing, moving forward, opening up the conversation and dancing.

DANCING WITH SETBACKS

i.e. my photographer, Amber, asking Brissa first

I think that's another notion – the way we deal with apparent setbacks. There are things that happen that are not quite what we want or expect. Learn how to dance with them, instead of taking them as rejections or at their face value. It helps to believe that there is a reason for whatever's thrown at you, so whatever you call a ball – whatever – just dance with it, and keep going, and stay in the flow. I know some of us have had tragic and horrible experiences. I believe that each of those experiences helps us to learn something we needed to learn. They can open us to welcoming others into our lives, they can lead us to be grateful for what we already have, to be present to the small miracles in life, or to become a major force in the world to lead or teach others. Your experience can help others. I believe there are no accidents in life! Say to yourself: 'OK, this is happening. All right. All right. Let me see what kind of dance... what's next. What can I do?' Just keep your mind open, and this will attract more good things if you welcome them in your life. Then ride that wave!

SUPPORT WHEN IT'S NEEDED

I lost my job on Monday afternoon and it's now Friday morning, and I have to admit that I've had my ups and downs. Part of me is already panicking and thinking, 'Oh my God! Da-da-da-daaaaa, da-da-da-daaaaa...!' Going down that route is dangerously seductive, but I'm constantly pulled back by the CCOR community members who've seen the 'I've Lost My Job' video. They're really supporting me – sending me messages that I receive daily – so that's very, very much helping to continue to see the light, even in this moment. I think it's important for all of us to have the support of people like that, so again, if you're searching for a job, you might want to be part of a positive community where you just tell things as they are, and receive support.

JUST RELAX!

It's important to come out and just say what's so, but then re-create, constantly re-create, and remind yourself of what's possible, and that it can be easy and effortless if you allow it to be. I cannot emphasise too much that it's a matter of getting out of the way and letting things unfold for you. Life can really take care of things, if you just relax and focus on your intention of finding a job that fully corresponds to your being. When you wake up in the morning you should focus on feeling truly blessed. Things will then manifest.

DEALING WITH THE NEWS

There's so much fear around unemployment and the economic situation right now that it's creating unnecessary worries inside of us. If you can focus on 'all is well' you will attract some new ideas about what you should be doing. When you turn on the radio, or open the newspaper, or talk to friends, you may get the impression that everyone is worried, and this then contributes to making you worried, and then you're away in that negative spiral. I find myself tending that way on occasion, despite my familiarity with the Law of Attraction, so I'm reminding myself again that there are some tremendous opportunities out there, and if I allow things to happen, they can effortlessly, but I must focus on 'all is well'… and it really is! When I hear the news I get pretty panicked. I'm very aware of what's happening. For example, there are about 300,000 French people in London. The ones who made the most money here, working as traders in the City, are now going back to France. This is hardly surprising, considering that they will be getting all the benefits from having lost their jobs here in the UK, and they'll be paid over there up to 75% of what they earned here. Yes, no wonder so many are going back!

RESISTING THE TEMPTATION TO RUN BACK TO MOM

When I hear this alarming news part of me thinks, 'OK, should I go back to France, and go and live with my mother? That way, the money that I was given for this month by the company I worked with would go much further than if stayed in this city with its exorbitant rents.' But at the same time, I would have to leave this city, and I don't really want to do that. I feel I need to be here. However, I am considering it because I would still be able to write the book and do the things that I need to do in relation to websites etc., and maybe I could put my stuff in storage here? Again I'm asking for higher guidance to know which way I should go. I know I have my little guardian angel here with me, and I hope that I shall be able to make the right decision. Thank you for the guidance that will come.

I'm so aware how easy it is to panic when you read the papers. I must put that tendency to one side and ask myself honestly whether moving back to France will ultimately help me and make me feel good? It would probably just delay some things. Yes, it would provide a nice comfortable cushion for a while, but I don't think a place of comfort would be the most productive for me. Having said that, then, I think I should stay in London and really *be* in this beautiful city, be part of this reality – what's really happening – because so much is happening here. Frankly, when I'm in Nantes at my mother's place – a tempting prospect – it just won't help me achieve my dreams. I think a lot of us have similar temptations. To give in to them doesn't help us tap into our creativity. I shall certainly discuss the possibility of returning to France with my mom, but I think I should stay in London, to keep that sense of urgency, and stay in the flow of things here, and make it happen, and make it happen fast.

TITHING

I have *The Secret Daily Teachings*, which is a spin-off book from the movie *The Secret*, containing teachings for every day of the year. Today, Friday (my Day 19 of those daily teachings), it says that one of the biggest things you can do to change your financial circumstances is to take 10% of what you receive and give it away. This is called the spiritual law of tithing, and it is supposedly the most powerful action you can take to bring more money into your life. Wow! Well, just thinking about that… I'm going to give 10% of what I'll receive for the month ahead (for the next three weeks now). I'm just going to give it away, not even knowing if I'm going to have enough for myself. What a quantum leap of faith – and I am going to do it! I'm committed to doing it. It's really hard for me to let go of that money, not having any security myself, but I am fully aware and want to play this 100% – to have the Law of Attraction and the Law of Tithing, or whatever it's called, on my side – so I'm going to do it and give 10% away.

Now, the question is: to whom and for what? Maybe I should actually start the foundation I've always wanted to start – a foundation to help young children see the world – or maybe I should find an organisation or somebody who already does that? I need to look into it but, regardless of what I'll do with it, this money needs to go away. I'm going to have to find a channel, a way for giving, whether it's to an individual or an organisation. Again, I'm asking for higher guidance, to show me who can benefit the most from this.

CERTAINTY ABOUT LONDON

Of course, I need to be in London! Of course I need to stay! Only ten minutes ago I was verging on thinking that leaving would be best. You know, this world is accelerating right now and sometimes we have a rush of ideas and fears. It's important to step back, and be with it, and not take any major decision within 24 hours, I would say. Let it sink in and ask, 'What would be best?' Staying in London for me right now is probably best. By staying here, I feel I tap into this power that I have, into the remarkable resources and potential we are all given at birth!

It's easy to be positive when everything is perfect. It's easy to stay in a positive frame of mind, but we're not talking here of wishful or positive thinking. We're talking of consciously applying the Law of Attraction at a time when it is really needed. The energy, the creative flow, and your power, is really the current that drives things, and for me that is just stronger in the city. London will enable me to tap into my power and find my dream job. My dream job is here. I have to have faith that things are going to happen, and that I will receive the help and guidance I need. It can happen fast if I allow it to.

NOTIONS OF TIME AND MONEY, AND MORE THOUGHTS ON LONDON / NANTES

We have to learn how to deal with that kind of time pressure and understand that there is not actually such a thing as time, or, in other words, that you can expand time and that you can attract things very fast... that you can stretch time so that you have enough time for everything. In other words our notions of time and finance have to shift radically. I know this is hard. I'm really struggling with it myself right now. I'm having a hard time to see how the money in my account can stretch so that I can have enough to pay the bills and move forward with my life long enough for things to kick in. However, the Law of Attraction, and my whole spiritual being, and everything that I have inside, tell me that there is more, that there's something that I need to do, and that I need to stay here. I need to stay in London. I need to be part of the city and really see what's happening here instead of hiding, going on a little hideaway-holiday with my parents. I can continue to write this book from here. I can continue to flow with the city so it will flow even stronger.

Yes, Nantes is a beautiful city and all. Yes, Mom has a gorgeous house, but it's like a little cocoon. Oh yes, she would cook for me, and I would have pleasant afternoons when I would quietly type into my computer the things that go through my mind, and I would have time to read, but the pace would be much slower, and here it's about urgency. It's about really doing something for the world. It's about doing something for my community at CCOR. It's about finding a new stream of income. It's… I think for me it's about being self-employed again. I have tears in my eyes, because I remember the last time I was self-employed – the ups and downs – but I was making a living. Not enough for the type of living that I wanted, though, whereas here, working for someone… Well, there's been security, but on the other hand, it just did not correspond fully with who I am. So I am taking on that risk and challenge again. I'm 31 and alone. I have no family and no kids. The positive side of this is that the situation is so much clearer: I really need to face reality and go for what feels good for me.

There are some amazing possibilities out there, working from home and doing contracts for various people. I know I can find several revenue streams, but if I did that from France, it would drive my mom crazy. At least, in the UK, I can have a good little set-up and be very careful and responsible about my spending.

A ONE-PAGE DECLARATION

I should stick with the thought that I am provided for – that it's my birthright – and just let the abundance come. To help me do this I'll be working on creating a declaration for myself, a one-pager. I encourage you to do the same. You simply declare on one page what your life is like and how you will feel in the future. For example, I shall declare something like:

I live in the context of joy and love and purpose, and things
flow naturally and effortlessly. Ideas come to me, and every

day I receive higher guidance on decisions, and this will
continue to be so.

You get the idea? I may share my full declaration in this diary once I've completed it. Yup. If you focus on neediness and lack, then you're going to find these everywhere, so I choose to see things as evidence of abundance, although I might need help right now. I admit to being scared of not having enough, which I think is understandable in a city like London.

LONDON DOESN'T HAVE TO BE EXPENSIVE

But, you know, that's my perception of London – that it's an expensive city. Is this really my perception, however, or is this just me automatically recycling received opinion? When I interrogate myself a bit more about this, I find I actually don't think it's really like that – or necessarily has to be like that. I have discovered that there are many things that you can do in London for very little; it doesn't have to be an expensive city! So I should be aware, from moment to moment, of how I view London. I resolve to see it as an amazing opportunity, where everything flows abundantly to me – occasions to party, vacations with friends, support from people, ways of doing things without having to spend.

ANOTHER POSSIBILITY FOR THE MEDITATION CD

I haven't had a response from Gary to date. Frustrated, I sent an email to Chris Dines whom I met in London several weeks ago. He's the author of *Power, Love, and Abundance*, he used to be a DJ and he has lots of contacts in the recording industry. He might be able to help.

THE MASTER SALAD

I just made this amazing salad. I'm going to call it the Master Salad because it's really good and it's nourishing my body. It feels so good! Basically, it's just what I had in the fridge and it's turned out excellent. I almost always put lettuce in my salads, but this one has no lettuce. It has about half an orange pepper in it, thinly sliced. It contains a full avocado. There's a little bit of green pepper. It has some sprouted organic peas, bean sprouts and chickpea sprouts (the last two come together in a ready-prepared mix). There's also some linseed, spring onions, and Greek olives (kalamata). To this I've added some olive oil, cider vinegar and Himalayan salt. It's just really, really, really good, and it's definitely nourishing my body.

BE INFORMED BUT BE SELECTIVE ABOUT YOUR SOURCES OF INFORMATION

While I'm eating my salad I'm reading some news from Pierre Jovanovic. It's in French and contains some really useful information about what's going on in the world – things that the popular local media are not telling us. It's quite negative, but I really want to face reality as long as I learn about it from a reliable source – not directly and solely from the mainstream media. Jovanovic acts as an intelligent filter, selecting a range of articles from the global media and putting another perspective on what's happening in the world. This is both interesting and grounding for me, and I think I need it. As an example, I'm now watching an RT video of an interview with Gerald Celente titled 'Worst economic collapse ever'. Have a look, it's fascinating: http://digg.com/world_news/Worst_economic_collapse_ever_Gerald_Celente.

THE LAW OF ATTRACTION DOES NOT MEAN AVOIDING REALITY

The Google keyword research I did the other day was a milestone for me, the wake-up moment when I came to realise what is really going on. I hadn't been looking before; I'd been in my own little bubble of positivity! Now that I've become aware of things, I'm reading one of the greatest blogs out there to fully inform myself, to be grounded in reality, yet still move forward. The Law of Attraction is not about avoiding reality but about facing it. From there you can really 'own' your power – who you really are – and create magnificence, and be there for others.

I'm not saying simply 'follow the media', because I think the mainstream popular media are all… Well, let's just say that they only say what they want to! No, I advise you to seek alternative sources of information, for example find a blog in your own language, written by a journalist who brings together information from multiple sources around the world. That's the sort of thing that's useful. Tap into the international news and see for yourself what's really happening instead of just waiting for the local media to package it for you. A good example of the sort of thing I mean is the video I was just watching of the Gerald Celente interview, a trend forecaster who's been making accurate predictions for years.

THE HUMAN REVOLUTION IS DUE

This is a really, really tough time we're going through. A lot is happening, and a lot more is going to happen. A while ago there was the Internet revolution, and I think something similar is going to happen now, something that will help us get out of our present predicament. Personally, I believe it's going to be the human revolution. There's a lot to be said about it. A month or two ago I had the idea of writing a book on the theme 'dare to declare', along the lines of Barack

Obama's *The Audacity Of Hope*, only it would explicitly demonstrate that we're now in an era when the discoveries with the most impact are going to be about human development rather than technology. Several things are pointing towards this.

What do I mean? I think society should be concerned, first and foremost, with what it takes to be a fully actualised human being. We should all be living to our full potential, using all our abilities and not just those we were been brought up to be aware of, but also this whole energy field, the power of our thoughts, the Law of Attraction… call it what you will. This book will, I trust, open your eyes to what is possible when you do think at that cutting edge. It should demonstrate how incredibly, how wonderfully, synchronicity happens, in such a magical way, and how it unfolds into a juicy living! A life of passion and purpose.

ATTRACTING MONEY FOR A MAC

I would like to attract the money to buy a new iMac 24"; this is money that's additional to the money I'm receiving from work, additional money that I'll be able to spend on this beautiful Mac. I think the Mac is about £1,300 or something, so I need to attract maybe £1,500 to allow me to get all the necessary peripherals also, which will include a desk. I declare to the universe I'm attracting £1,500 out of nowhere. I should add that this money is coming to me to enable me to buy this iMac in order that I can write the book. I shall be able to do the research I need, and all the editing of videos, uploading etc., and it'll lead me to be creative and enjoy 110% the development process of the book and projects to come!

HAPPILY HUNG OVER, AND MORE THOUGHTS ON THE BOOK

Boy, I'm hung over after last night. It was my company leaving-do, and also Richard's birthday (the company COO). It was so much fun, but I had way too many glasses of red wine! I got the chance to have a great conversation with my colleagues (well, ex-colleagues now!), and I found out that Marc Holland, a real talent when it comes to design, does some work on the side, so I can hire him to do the cover of the CD and that of the book. I'm super, super excited to have met him. So that's one thing ticked off.

I've also been in touch with Rebecca Lori (www.littlebombay. co.uk) who used to work for the company as well. When I became redundant I contacted her and asked if she could do some editing for me, because she's a great editor, so I might not need to go down the route with Stephanie over in New York. We'll see. It will depend how things come together, but I definitely have options at my fingertips now, and I just love it. I really love it. I have been feeling profoundly blessed from the moment I woke up this morning. Yes, with a hangover, but just so grateful for everything that has happened, and for the fact that I can now create anything that I want. It's really up to me, and I just love that. It's so empowering.

GOD HAS A BIGGER SHARE IN MY LIFE NOW

So I thank Life and I find myself more faithful. It's as if God has a bigger share of my life now, and I really appreciate that. I'm so thankful for the opportunity of practising, to the fullest extent, the implementation of the Law of Attraction (one of the set of Universal Laws or 'laws that govern the universe'). I'm thankful to have opened my eyes to the reality of things in the world, because it gives me more power.

I am talking for the power of the heart here. The power to help others, the confidence to encourage a stranger, the willingness to make a difference, the surrendering, the ongoing joy and fulfilment that Life can bring. I am talking about our 'Self' expressing itself as Life flow through us.

KNOWLEDGE IS POWER

Yesterday, I made another video on the Law of Attraction. It's different from positivity, you know. There's a misconception that the Law of Attraction is positive thinking, or wishful thinking. It's not. Even I used to practise it, thinking, 'Oh, I need to be positive, so the less I know what's happening in the world, the better.' In fact, I am discovering that you really get your power from seeing things as they are, and then declaring what you want. This approach has a far more solid foundation than mere wishful thinking. It's much more powerful.

MY DREAM OF HELPING CHILDREN SEE THE WORLD

I want to help thousands of children travel so that they can discover the world. It's one of the things I've always wanted to do – start a foundation that will help kids travel. You see, I think I was blessed at a young age to grow up in both France and the USA, and to hold dual citizenship. This experience opened me to the world, and to people. I feel at home pretty much everywhere I go. I'm not afraid of differences, because I was exposed to different cultures, values and ways of thinking at a very young age. I get along with people from all kinds of backgrounds. I want to give that experience of travel to kids whose parents (or guardians) can't afford to. I want to give them the opportunity to see something new, to see other countries, to go to Asia, Africa, the USA... That should really make a difference to their lives and be something for them to look forward to and aim for, something that will open their eyes and give them the motivation to reach for their dreams. I say Yes to that!

EMPHASISING THE IMPORTANCE OF GRATITUDE

I just saw a Louise Hay video on YouTube in which she talks about how our thoughts create our reality (http://www.youtube.com/watch?v=58f-RHI3UUM). I just love Louise Hay. She is an amazing woman. I love her way of putting things.

One of the most powerful things is to be grateful for what we have, and for what we don't have: good or bad. _Life loves_ gratitude, as Louise Hay says. Notice that there is always something to be grateful for. Notice the shift of your energy when you recognise this. Just thinking about it makes me relax. You?

I am blessed. Yes, I am so grateful that I lost my job and that I've been given this opportunity to live my dream now. I'm grateful for having a roof over my head. I'm grateful for my friends. I'm grateful for the '100-Day Reality Challenge' community. I'm grateful for all the people I've attracted into my life. I'm grateful for needing to eat healthily. I'm grateful for having been introduced many years ago to the Law of Attraction. I'm grateful for having this opportunity to write this book. I'm grateful for it being sunny today. I'm grateful for having a cozy bed. I'm grateful for… I'm grateful for…

I used to have my own company, yes, but I would treat it as if it were just another job that served to pay the bills. I would design websites and do Internet marketing for various US companies, but that wasn't my dream job – it used to be!

I do love to travel. In fact, one of the reasons I started an Internet company after September 11 (9-11) was to be able to work from anywhere in the world, and I subsequently did work in various places. But my soul really started to sing when, in 2005, I co-founded the '100-Day Reality Challenge'. From that point on I would work weekends and evenings improving the 'Co-Creating Our Reality' website, promoting the '100-Day Reality Challenge', and making YouTube videos. At this stage it became clear that my 'real' job was not as fulfilling, and I was a coward in that I didn't fully admit to this sooner. I would not say that I entirely wasted four years of my life, but I am certainly looking forward to discovering what my dream job is!

Deepak Chopra describes this eloquently in *The Seven Spiritual Laws of Success* (I love that book!). The seventh law, the Law of 'Dharma', says that everyone has a purpose in life, a unique gift that we need to express and put our whole heart into. If we do not, then we rot from the inside out, and start 'stinking up our souls'! (These are not Deepak's words but Brian Johnson's, in his 22-minute mp3 summary of Deepak's book.)

So, for the first time in my life, I'm going to focus on what I truly love 100% of the time.

Just because I believe that fulfilment for me lies in being self-employed doesn't mean that you can't create something wonderful while working for someone else; such a situation could truly be a blessing in one's life.

I'm so grateful, however, to realise that I am now able to focus on going forward despite the little voice that sometimes pops up and says, 'Let's just design websites for companies. It pays well.' Yes, I know I could easily find people who want this service, and make money doing it, but it would lead me off the road I have chosen and on which I can truly express what I am uniquely good at. I am grateful for having had this opportunity to wake up to my dreams, and to wake other people to theirs.

Get ready for miracles, guys! This journey is going to unfold. It's unfolding right now!

LESSONS

I learned so many things in my current job – I mean in my previous job! – that I needed to learn. For instance, that I can't do everything on my own! The list is actually quite a long one. I am going to put it together here, right now, and I suggest you do something similar – list the lessons you have learnt from some job or particular experience, for which you are very grateful. So here are some things that I wouldn't have learnt without my last job:

- *I've learned how to organise my ideas more efficiently.*

- *I've deepened my knowledge of how the travel and hotel industry works.*

- *I've mastered Google Analytics, which is a wonderful website tracking tool.*

- *I've learned to be more detailed and precise.*

- *I've learned how to communicate more effectively with my peers, managers and small groups of people*

- *I've learned humility, although I always had a big ego and still do. As my boss would say, 'a rough diamond'!*

- *I've learned that we are all specialists with regard to something, and that I don't need to have it all myself. I can count on others.*

- *I've learned that one can achieve much more when working as part of a team.*

- *I realised Internet marketing was not my passion.*

- *I think I've learned to be a better person, more rounded than I was before.*

- *I'm also grateful because the job brought me to the UK. Did I say I love living in London?*

IMAGINE PERFECT TIMING

I'm walking home (I live just off Abbey Road), having done some grocery shopping. It's a beautiful sunny day today. I'm passing the Beatles' studio – 5 Abbey Road – on the wall of which 'Imagine' is written. IMAGINE. I long felt drawn to living near here, an urge I felt every time I walked past the studio. It's inspiring to be reminded constantly that those guys came here to record. Every day now hundreds of people come here – by day, by night, come rain, come shine – they all come to see the famous Abbey Road studio, and to write their little notes on the wall, notes of gratitude, acknowledging what a difference the Beatles made. I like this part of London. St John's Wood is very elegant. But I am moving to Earl's Court on Friday. I relish the feeling of 'newness' it will give me. I love moving, and changes, and packing – starting afresh. It's a great opportunity. Perfect timing. Couldn't be better. I think it's important to get to an emotional place where we can acknowledge that everything that's happened to us is perfectly timed, even something to be grateful for.

I'm home now.

'VISION BOARDING' FOR A 24" IMAC

I love creating vision boards because it really helps me to visualise – to *feel* – what I want to attract, and also to get clearer on what I want to experience. Right now I want to attract a 24" iMac, which I just checked is around £1,200, so I want to attract £1,500 (to allow for extras), or the iMac itself. I'm very open as to how it will come, but however it comes I think I'll feel wonderful; I'll certainly be able to make great progress with everything to do with this project. For that reason I want to attract it quickly. Creating a vision board will speed the process. I visualise myself typing away on it, and surfing the web, and really loving the experience, awed by how fast the computer is. I feel gratitude for having this Mac in front of me soon... It's about getting my emotions to that place right now.

DECLARING THAT I'LL MAKE A GREAT LIVING FROM DOING WHAT I LOVE

I can do anything I want right now, in this freed-up time and space, so let me remind myself to focus on finding not just any kind of job but my dream job. What could this look like? What is a dream job for me? What are the things that I love in life? I love to plan things such as social events. I love getting people together. I love social communities. I love hosting events, and interviewing people on camera. I love doing videos on YouTube. I love inspiring people, and, now that I think of it, these are things that I've never given 100% to. I always had another job, even when I was self-employed. I was never focused on my passions. I was doing website design and Internet marketing to earn my living, but 'Co-Creating Our Reality' and the YouTube videos and the amateur TV show I did in Chicago were always jobs on the side. I never said, 'I can make a living from this.' Far less did I have the guts to say, 'I'm *going* to make a living from this!' I think that's the crucial shift, and when it happens, when you realise that *this* is what you want to do for the rest of your life – that you *deserve* to have such wonderful, fulfilling work – then there's something there.

I'm wondering why I settled for that. Perhaps it was because I was afraid to give my all to the things I loved, because if I failed I would have felt devastated? I think the explanation must lie along those lines.

I think I was waiting for the perfect moment to come. I was waiting for a miracle – to be picked up by a television producer who would sweep me off on a white horse, and life would be good ever after.

So now, I declare that, yes, I can make a living (and a beautiful, great living at that!) from doing the things I love. This is what I want. I've never declared this before today. I never took full ownership of this to this day. I've always been cowed by that whingeing voice in the back of my head: 'Oh, yeah, but I really need to pay the bills so I need a normal job.' No longer. I'm done with that, and now I can fully live my passion.

REIKI CURES HANGOVERS, AND MORE!

I just did a 20-minute reiki quickie on myself. It was very beneficial. I spent five minutes on each of the energy points. My hangover is gone now, I feel much better, and I'm off to the gym. If you don't know about reiki, you might want to check it out. It's a healing technique. It would be better if you had it done to you (all good spas have it as part of their list of treatments now) rather than me try to explain it, but the gist of it is that it's to do with energy, and that it helps to rebalance and harmonize your body. When I went to a spa I always asked for 30 minutes of reiki and 30 minutes of deep tissue massage, to get the best of both worlds. I have been a certified 'Reiki 1' practitioner since January. I thought it would help me to balance my energy, counteracting the effects of the negative environment I was working in at the time.

It feels so good, and it can definitely rid you of a hangover, or a headache, or stress, or what have you. It's Japanese – yup, they know a lot of stuff! I love it. I'm going to go to Japan one day.

PROMPTED TO BUY *THE ARTIST'S WAY*

I'm on Amazon at the moment, buying the book called *The Artist's Way*, because I have just heard about it three times in quick succession. When this sort of thing happens, I take action. That was what motivated me to move to Chicago; the third time one of my very good friends, Sandra, told me explicitly that this was a city truly made for me. So I went there to check it out. So many signs were pointing in that direction.

I knew I had to move there when I saw the place. My friend Hank had picked me up in his new and flamboyant raspberry Cadillac convertible (he lives a couple of hours from Chicago in Michigan) and we cruised (as we say in the USA) on Michigan Avenue (Chicago's Champs Elysées), and along Lake Shore Drive, on this beautiful and sunny day of August 2006. I loved everything about it (well, apart from those yellow taxis honking all the time and for no apparent reason). Twenty-four hours in the city was enough for me to make my mind up. I had heard about the long, windy and cold winters, but I thought, 'Well, I want change, and have been asking for change'. Miami had become too dull and predictable. I was longing for culture, and felt something bigger was waiting for me there. So I moved!

The same feeling applies to this book I'm buying right now. It's supposed to help you be more creative, and gives you little exercises to do every day, so I believe there is a reason for me being inspired to buy it. The final prompt I needed came today, when I received an email from a friend telling me that her book is the fourth best seller on Amazon. I clicked on the link she sent, and on the same web page I saw *The Artist's Way*! Exciting!

PART-TIME WORK: FOCUS GROUPS AND USABILITY TESTING

As I was doing a YouTube search on job loss, I came across a video of someone talking about experiencing the loss of a job. He mentioned things like getting unemployment benefit. I didn't like the connotation of this – that I might be out of work for some time – but it did give me the idea that I could also participate in focus groups. I would quite like to do a few little part-time things (not requiring too much commitment, just to earn a bit of cash), and I am certainly interested in the areas of focus groups and usability testing. (Usability testing is what's done to websites before they go public.) Usually they run in the evenings too, which suits me fine.

I contacted the company that did the usability testing for my last employer's website, and I've offered my services to them. They'll at least put me on their database. After that I searched for focus groups in London and I found somewhere that's always looking for new people. I submitted my profile, which took two minutes, and now I wait to hear from them.

As you can see, I'm creating all these little income streams, placing the ball wherever I feel inspired to, and it feels great, so why not? Why not send an email, or call and see what's going on, see what's possible? I think, though, that in order to harvest these types of ideas we need to say to ourselves: 'OK, I'm open to it.' Only then do things start happening. I have to confess, though, that I am not fully enthused about doing a part-time job. But what is good is that it did not take long, and keeps me in the flow.

DEFINING MY DREAM JOB

Setting the little things to the side, I'm clear that I want to manifest my dream job, and this is a big, bold statement. I have to define it a bit, to be clear that I'm fully aligned, and that I know what I want to manifest. For me, my dream job is a job that I completely love, that I enjoy every day, that is fully on purpose, and that helps me develop my skills by virtue of the fact that I love it. I shall wake up every morning excited and thankful to be able to generate income this way. It's a job in which I shall earn at least what I was earning in my last position, so a nice salary as a minimum. I reckon this will grow exponentially, but at the beginning, to declare it – to make it concrete – I'll say that it's a real job bringing me at least the same money as my last one. The amount that I'll be making will enable me to have a good lifestyle, such that I don't need to make compromises. I shall enjoy all the luxuries that I love, and the money will just flow in. I'll be able to help others... Anyway, to repeat: my target, to kick things off, is to make at least what I was making in my previous position.

YOUTUBE PARTNER PROGRAMME

I have, of course, long since planted the seeds I shall now be focusing on cultivating. We all have hobbies and things that we love and, frankly, I think it's pretty easy to start generating some supplementary income from them. What I want to discuss is how I am going to create some additional streams of income while I'm still working on refining my definition of my dream job... while things are shaping. I want to feel good. I want money to start coming in. I think we can all do with some extra cash, right?

I've been part of the YouTube programme (http://www.youtube.com/partners) since 2008. For everybody who clicks on an ad next to one of my videos, I get a small fee. It works the same way as Google Adsense (actually the YouTube programme is linked to Adsense). The revenues I generate from it have been building. At present I'm probably averaging 3,000 - 5,000 video views a day. When the quality of the content improves the number of views increases, so by putting more effort into this, I should be able to go from making maybe $350 a month from YouTube videos to five times that, or, at least, triple the amount, but my goal should really be to increase it exponentially, because there are some guys on YouTube, such as Michael Buckley with his show *What the Buck?* (http://www.youtube.com/user/whatthebuckshow), who are making a fortune. He's very funny, very gay, and speaks very fast. He's just hilarious! He started doing his show, in which he gossips about celebrities, on top of his main job. I believe he bought a camera for $2,000. (You don't need to spend that kind of money. I think a Flip camera is a good option and provides a satisfactory image, and that's what I use. The Flip is so easy to use! I carry it everywhere. And then you need good lighting, and you're away!) Michael also has a backdrop, which is probably a good idea, and something that I should consider, but, anyway, my point is that he's starting to make some serious money – $100,000 a year with his videos – and now it's his full-time job. Yes, I'm definitely going to go down that route and do more videos and boost my earnings on the YouTube partner programme! Now that's something that I love doing: video diaries!

MORE ABOUT MONEY FROM EVENTS

Another idea I had for creating an additional income stream was to organise events. I'd love to create more events here in London. I've done a few free singles' events with the help of my delicious British friend Patrick Drake, but, to tell you the truth, it doesn't feel right for me to start charging singles to meet, so I think I'll continue to make them free, but perhaps I could look for income from negotiating something with a club when I take people along? I think that's called a club promoter. Yes, I'll definitely be exploring that.

I love bringing people together, so another angle on the singles scene, one I mentioned before, would be to organise some long-weekend getaways for singles out of London. This would certainly be fun!

THE DECISION TO SELF-PUBLISH

I've decided to self-publish this book. There is no need for me to find a publisher. This is something I have been considering over the last few days, and I think I'm getting clear now that I want to self-publish.

Regardless of whether I self-publish or not, I'll still have to put a solid book proposal together. A book proposal is more or less a business plan that spells out the target market, the marketing strategy – a detailed plan of actions to promote the book. It's clearly useful to do, and probably even more important when you're self-publishing. So although I'm self-publishing I'm still going to put that together.

The good thing about publishers is that they sometimes give you an advance (money!) when they see potential in your manuscript, but apparently this is quite rare these days, and they are giving out less. Then they expect you to do all the marketing yourself, so, I have to ask what can they do that I haven't already got in hand? I have potentially found somebody to help me edit the book, and Marc Holland could handle all the artwork, such as the book cover. So all that's left is the marketing, which I have gained experience in, over the past eight years.

Laura Duksta, who wrote a very successful children's book called *I Love You More*, has a lot of experience in self-publishing, so I can also ask her, but I think these days for something like this to work it has to become viral, so I need to operate fast, and to operate fast I need to remove one of the links in the supply chain, which is the publisher. Yes, publishers help you get your book into stores, but a lot of people now buy online, and since my natural market is online – I've always been online – I may as well stay online. The other good thing about cutting out a publisher is that you make more money per book sold. Publishers only pass on a tiny percentage of the cover price of every copy, and I want to sell this book for less than £10 ideally ($11-12). It should be easily affordable so that people don't have to think twice about buying it. What I'm looking for is volume sales to get the message out there. So, taking everything into account, self-publishing is definitely the way to go, especially for this first one, and especially considering the current economic climate when publishers are a bit chilly. That's my decision made!

ADVERTISING FOR A TRANSCRIPTION TYPIST

OK, I'm posting an ad on Gumtree in the UK (the equivalent of Craig's List in the USA) because I've realised that typing up what I've been recording on my iPhone just doesn't feel right. I feel I'm wasting my time, although I know that theoretically I have the time to do it, and part of me wants to do it, but it could be done by someone who needs a job, who might just need the extra cash. Possibly even the information that he or she might pick up could be of benefit! I want to be able to attract a person I can trust completely, someone who will do a great job at typing this up quickly. It wouldn't require any writing skills, per se. So I'm posting the ad now. From now on, then, I'll be just working on the typed notes, editing and reorganising them to some extent. After that, I'll take it to yet another level, because I know that as I'm recording this, talking into the Dictaphone as thoughts occur to me, it's a long way from good prose, and I probably won't be able to polish it properly myself. I want to keep the tone of it, but maybe a person in the UK or in the USA will be able to edit it further?

REBECCA TRIGGERS MORE IDEAS ABOUT THE BOOK

I just received an email from Rebecca who worked for the same company as me but lost her job a month before I did. She happens to be a great editor. I replied, asking if she would be interested in editing the content.

FASHION WEEK: FUN, CREATIVITY, EMACIATED MODELS AND A HELPFUL CONVERSATION

I'm going to a Fashion Week show at 3 p.m. Oh my God, it's already 2.25! Time is flying by. I just love it! Oh, but I want to do my hair and everything! Drat! I'd better just go.

I just came back from the fashion show. It was a lot of fun, with cameras everywhere. Exciting to see the creativity of those clothes designers, but, boy, were those models super-skinny! I thought they were going to faint. Honestly, I've never seen creatures so emaciated in my life. It's just ridiculous; I can't imagine that they're happy. The look on their face was empty. I did not see any life there. Maybe this was what they were instructed to do, but I can tell you there was no spark in their eyes! I wonder how our society got that far down the rabbit hole?

Anyway, it was fun for me, and I had a great conversation with Henrik, my future flatmate. We talked about possibilities on the work front, and where he's at at the moment. It was a very healthy, real conversation that helped me firm up my ideas and priorities.

SELF-EMPLOYED OR NOT?

Before going to sleep last night, I spent a few minutes doing some reiki on myself, and then I asked to receive higher guidance during my sleep. New ideas have certainly arrived; I'm wondering about creating content for a Web TV channel. On the other hand, in a way I do this already with my own videos on the YouTube partner programme, and I'm making money from it, but it's possibly worth looking into the possibilities and practicalities of this other option. I'm not sold on it. I'm not convinced I would like working for an Internet TV company. The more I think about it, the more I think being self-employed is really the right thing for me. I'm more productive, more alive, more creative.

STAYING IN THE FLOW

I must acknowledge that part of me is worried: how am I going to generate revenue right now? I must have faith in the process. Any negative thing can be turned into positive, so focus on the positive and good things will start to materialise! This has been my experience in the past, and it's the beginning of a new adventure now. It's been only a week, and I want to continue on a high and keep the energy. The more I feel uncertain of the future, the more I have to apply all those practices that I know to be effective.

I'm creating the possibility of a productive and beautiful day, in which I'm fully in harmony with my higher Self and am guided to each successive step, in the knowledge that I will be provided for, and that I don't have to worry about money concerns and others fears popping up.

AN EMAIL FROM THE CO-CEO OF WAYN

I just received an email. This one was from Jerome Touze, who is the Co-CEO of WAYN (Where Are You Now, http://www.wayn.com). I don't know if you've heard of this friend-locating/social-networking website? Anyway, I talked to him at my last singles event. I had previously seen him speak at a couple of social media events that I went to in Germany a couple of months ago. Through the workings of the Law of Attraction (I have no doubt) he was one of the first people to walk into the singles event. We'll be having lunch together, he just confirmed, on the 5th of March, at which we'll chatting about the possibility of my creating a WAYN event in London, a subject we had broached earlier. He has this really charismatic energy to him, and I'm definitely interested in seeing how all this unfolds and learning from him.

I have no idea how this will all pan out in the end, but I'm definitely doing things that feel good and that are progressing.

GIVE ME THE BENEFIT OF THE DOUBT

At every crossroads, setback or stumbling block we should ask ourselves: 'OK, what's possible? How can I turn this into a positive experience?' It's a virtuous circle: the more we're in this mindset, the more we stay in this flow, the more energy we have, and the more ideas we generate. I'm just buzzing with new ideas, and I think it's due to the fact that I haven't stopped to give myself time to slip into a 'poor me' mode of thinking. I lost my job a week ago, and it would have been all too easy to despair about how I would get by: 'Life is screwed up, and I'm worthless! I'm not going to be able to find another job now because of the economy...' The more we think this way, the less likely it is that we will attract a dream job, so we might as well try a different approach.

Try something new. Give me the benefit of the doubt, and test it out! If you can get to the point of starting to feel good, in full awareness of what has happened to you, then good things will happen. It's not about denying reality, and trying to be positive for the sake of being positive, while, deep down, you feel 'yucky', and have doubts etc. No, it's about genuinely feeling good.

FOCUS ON WHAT IS POSSIBLE, AND ASK, IF NECESSARY

The idea here is to focus on what is possible. We should ask ourselves: 'What can I do? How can I discover something that I can do and that I would really enjoy doing every day?' If you're not quite there yet – if you still have some resentment or some negative energy – then just keep asking, 'What can I do? 'Please give me some signs!' or 'I'm asking for higher guidance. What is my next step here? How can I find joy again? What will provide joy in my work?' You get the idea, I am sure! Just don't stop at, 'Oh, this is it. I'm screwed!' With that outlook, nothing new will come to you. Those ideas will only flow if you start opening the valve, and if you start opening yourself: 'I'm open to receive… to being creative about this. I haven't made up my mind yet that this sucks.' If you say it sucks, then it's going to suck, and the experience of it is going to suck. If you say, that it's good, *and really believe that it's good*, then the experience is just so juicy, and so incredible… it's as if you have a new vantage point from which you can see so much better. Ideas will come together.

Like you I have my fears. We all do; even the person you admire and respect the most has fears. I personally have no idea how this is going to turn out right now. I'm going to have bills to pay. But I keep myself in that Law-of-Attraction state of mind through the practices I am mentioning.

A REMINDER ABOUT THE VISUALISATION CD

It's now 10.30. I just received this email:

> *I'm a fan of your meditations that I found on YouTube. I use them at work to help me get through the day. I just found something on the Law of Attraction meditation and the visualization CD on your web site. I'm interested in knowing how to obtain it. Can you please let me know where and how I can find it?*

I recorded these meditations last November with Gary, a South Florida music producer. It's a shame that nothing seems to have come of this, because I feel like I did a good job, but perhaps I should re-record it here in London and make it even better!

A FRENCH INSPIRATION

I've been looking at various books on Amazon.com to see which ones are closest to the one I want to do. I'm thinking of a diary style of book, a mix of narrative and practical exercises and advices. I just ordered a book called *Petit Cahier d'Exercices du Lâcher-Prise* from France that my friend Chantal recommended. I should receive it in three or four days. It sells for six or seven Euros and was published very recently (October 2008) by Jouvence, a major French publishing company. My impression is that it's more aligned with what I'd like to do than most other books out there. It seems playful and approachable. Definitely affordable!

A POSSIBLE APPEARANCE ON BBC RADIO 2

I just received an urgent inquiry from the Chris Evans show on BBC Radio 2:

> *Dear Lilou,*
> *Could you please get in touch with the Chris Evans show, on*
> *BBC Radio 2. We'd like to find out more about the 100-Day*
> *Reality Challenge. Give me a ring when you get this email.*

Ha, ha! How fun is that! I called them back, but apparently it was too late to speak to them today and I should call again tomorrow. One of their listeners told them about the '100-Day Reality Challenge'. I'll be contacting that person to thank her. Anyway, I emailed the BBC back with some more details about the community.

We have over 3,000 members in 125 countries to date. *The Oprah Winfrey Show* was interested in featuring us last year. Her show on the Law of Attraction featuring *The Secret* had been a real success. So Oprah decided to do more shows on the Law of Attraction. This is why her producers contacted us. Being THE community for living the Law of Attraction, one that has generated thousands of videos testifying to its power, they naturally had to call us! After weeks of reviewing hundreds of videos from participants, they selected 18 and put together a video montage. At the last minute, they decided not to feature it on the show. I have to confess that I have not given up on that idea, and have declared that we shall be featured on Oprah's show.

Anyway, I also told the BBC representative that I had lost my job and that I was in the process of attracting my dream job and doing some videos about the process, so maybe that'll be another thing of interest to them that we can perhaps speak about. I think it would be great to get the word out about this on radio.

MANIFESTING ERIC

Another little Law-of-Attraction story for you… I receive Google Alerts for my name so whenever my name is mentioned in Google or somebody mentions it in a blog, I'm notified. Today, I received an email saying that somebody mentioned my name. Sometimes I click on these alerts, sometimes I don't, but this time I did, and it directed me to a blog called 'biowrite.wordpress.com', and this is written by a gentleman by the name of Eric (well, actually, Dr. R. Eric Swanepoel), and here's what I read in the middle of one his postings:

An important spin-off benefit of reading literature dealing with the above topics (and, bien sûr, watching the ever-delightful Lilou Mace (http://www.liloumace.com/) was that I became qualified to help people write books on personal development and the like.

Now he mentioned my name, so I felt I had to read this, and then I discover that he helps authors. It's amazing! I imagine this guy will have the skill to take my memos to a whole other level. I sent him an email and thanked him for mentioning me in his blog, and, hopefully, he'll be excited about my project!

Now I'm off for a good workout at the gym where I'll also be meeting co-creator Sophia (http://www.cocreatingourreality.com/profile/SofiaBustamante), who contacted me through YouTube!

ELEVEN AGAIN!

Funny, it's 5.11. I have looked at my watch so many times only to see that there's an 11 after the hour. It was a strange feeling this time, but I love it. I feel very connected every time I see that. I feel on track.

MORE FROM ERIC'S BLOG

I'm looking a little bit more at Eric's blog. It discusses the Law of Attraction and mentions the movie, *The Secret*, and says how the Law of Attraction can be traced back to *The Science Of Getting Rich* and to the famous *Think and Grow Rich* by Napoleon Hill (which is a great book that I read some time ago) and he says:

> So what is 'the Law of Attraction'? According to the last link I gave you:

> 'The Secret of The Secret is to think positive thoughts: think that you have what you want to have all the time, visualise it, be grateful for it in advance and feel positive feelings as the thinking itself won't cut it without them. You have two sets of feelings: good feelings and bad feelings.'

And then he goes on in his blog:

> No discussion of this topic is complete without a mention of the charming Lilou Mace (www.liloumace.com) whose YouTube postings are a constant joy. Here (http://www.youtube.com/watch?v=FZZ5Ubj3uW0) she is discussing the difference between positive thinking and the Law of Attraction...

That's actually the video that I did two or three days ago, so he probably wrote this very recently!

> *…and here (http://www.youtube.com/watch?v=hwshffMkZPw)*
> *is her response to being sacked.*

Hah! That's another expression – 'to be sacked' – you know I keep on saying 'lost my job', and 'made redundant' – redundant. So: 'sacked'. Hah! I have more vocabulary now. I need to find many words for 'job loss' now. The people living in Alaska apparently have hundreds of words for snow. Perhaps I need hundreds of ways of saying 'I'm sacked', or 'I've lost my job'! So here's a new one for me.

How interesting is that! I've been reading a bit more on Eric's website (biowrite.co.uk), and at the end of a summary of all his writing activities he says:

> *I have discovered that I have a talent for bringing people's*
> *stories alive. I am passionate about such work and take pride*
> *in doing the best possible…*

I want to say 'joy' here, but the word he uses is 'job'. I'm sure he takes a lot of joy in it though! He continues:

> *My broad background in the sciences and arts, my*
> *international experience, and my contacts in various fields (the*
> *media, literature, music, science, education and politics) are all*
> *relevant to my work as a biographer. In assisting people with*
> *their biographies, I have found a field in which, as a generalist,*
> *I am ideally qualified to specialise. Try me!*

I'm going to try you. Yes, Eric. This is excellent, because not only are you a writer, but you seem to be specialising in writing biographies, which is more or less what this diary is – it's a personal journey. It's somebody's journey unfolding as they attract their dream job, so it seems that it would work really nicely. I'm looking forward to seeing what Eric can do!

MEETING SOPHIA: TITHING BECOMES EXCITING!

It's 10.30 p.m. I'm walking home from St John's Wood tube station, one of the last times I'll be doing this, as I won't be living at on Abbey Road much longer. I just met Sophia in the gym. She's a lovely British lady focused on community and on people really helping each other. She was telling how she's working with kids in the Brixton area of South London: 15- and 16-year-olds, youngsters who have been involved in gangs or who are at risk of being drawn into them. She's providing coaching and general support. I thought: 'What a fabulous project!' And then I thought, 'Well, there we go. Maybe that's it. Maybe I'll give the money I wanted to donate to a good cause to her, and that's the project I've been attracting.' As I was listening to her talking about it, I thought, 'How about providing those kids with some webcams, and offering them the opportunity of participating in the "100-Day Reality Challenge"?' I can buy some cameras, and all the equipment, journals, magazines and vision boards that they might need – everything – and then do an intro video, or meet them in person and offer them the opportunity of participating in the '100-Day Reality Challenge'. Perhaps this sort of experience could empower other kids all around the country? Yes, if it is successful this project could lay the foundations for something really big! How cool would that be? …And Sophia was very enthusiastic – 'Yeah, that would be fantastic!'

I'm so looking forward to this – it's so juicy, guys! It's amazing how life just unfolds when you let it – one thing after the next – just mind-blowing! There's another potential benefit to this too. Doing this project with south-side kids, and potentially transforming their lives, could increase the chances of Oprah featuring us on her show, so it's win-win-win all over the place! Yes, I think there's a good chance that Oprah will be interested in such a story! The youngsters won't even need to read *The Secret*. I can send them some YouTube links. There's plenty of free support out there. We already have the '100-Day Reality Challenge' website community in place: www.CoCreatingOurReality.com. We have Sophia, who is already a coach. I have hundreds of 'how-to' videos online… so there they go! Let's experiment with all this.

WHY CHILDREN SHOULD EXPERIENCE TRAVEL

It's Monday today, and I'm having the best week of my life. A week ago I had just announced that I had been sacked – my new word, ha, ha! – and here I am now getting involved in a project that could empower kids here in London, and potentially many more around the world. I was also able to tell Sophia about my dream of one day having a foundation to help young children see a bit of the world. I explained the impact that such an experience had had on me. In fact, although my parents are French and I spent most of my childhood in France, I was born in the USA and celebrated my first birthday in a plane! My parents took me travelling all over the world, and this was tremendously enriching. I think this is why I can now move around the world so easily, feeling at home everywhere, and why I am able to dream so big, and create so many things. I want others to have that same experience!

SABOTAGING THOUGHTS AND INSOMNIA

It's 4.15 a.m. and I can't sleep. I'm too excited about everything that is happening and, at the same time, a little worried. This is quite common when things starts manifesting like this. We're just not used to it in our day-to-day lives, so it's a little bit scary, and sometimes life

Affluence — flowing towards

seems to want to sabotage it. I have found myself in this situation more than once. It's as if when one has been in the flow for a while, part of one wakes up and says, 'Whoa! This is really happening!' and so this is such a time. I remind myself that it's important to just relax, to accept the good that I'm creating, and to let the natural flow continue. Things are supposed to be like that – flowing in. Breathing deeply, in and out, and cancelling my negative thoughts will help. I won't let them sabotage the good that's happening. Constantly re-creating what I am committed to is essential. Focusing on the good. Meditation really helps me with this. It's at least as important to practise meditation in the heat of things, when things are falling into place, as at the beginning when they are not. Right now, I am manifesting additional potential, additional income. I am manifesting a project to help kids who need it. I am manifesting the completion of the book. Focus, Lilou, breathe deeply, in and out, and accept.

I'm being grateful for all these things. One powerful way of getting back on track is simply to listen to one of the several guided visualisations that are now on the Internet. That really helps me release my fears and be present. I am now strongly considering recording some of my guided visualisations for a CD here in London. Each visualisation/ meditation will address a particular issue, so that you can choose one appropriate for your circumstances. All of them, fundamentally, will be about accepting good things in life – opening up to that good and welcoming it in. It's a beautiful thing. When you start getting used to it, you can remain in the flow, and try to expand the feeling. See how far you can take it.

AFFIRMATIONS

'All is good,' I tell myself, as I continue to breathe deeply, in and out. 'Yes, I want all those beautiful and amazing things to happen. Yes, I am grateful for this.'

You could write down a couple of affirmations like that for yourself, things that will help you continue to accept the challenge of making thing better. I just keep repeating: 'Yes, I want all those beautiful things to happen in my life. I'm so grateful for it all. Thank you.' I also ask for higher guidance to find a way of accepting all the things happening in my life. So, Life, please help me in accepting all this greatness that's happening!

MANIFEST WHAT YOU REALLY WANT NOW!

I'm still awake, and it's now 4.30 a.m. That worried voice is still there: 'Oh my God, is it really happening?' I think the right thing to do now is a meditation, and so I'm going to listen to my visualisation called *Effective Meditation | Manifest what you really Want NOW!* (http://www.youtube.com/watch?v=RQLXTF7FT_c). It's free. I'll listen to it now. It lasts about ten minutes and starts with simple deep breathing. Then my voice will guide me to accept all this goodness and love, and to continue to expand myself to receive it all…

BE AWARE, NOT AFRAID

From this morning I've been searching online for UK and US unemployment statistics. They're on the rise. The unemployment rate is 7.5 % in the USA right now – there are 11.6 million people out of work… and counting. The impact is reflected in blogs and press releases. Fear is growing, so, more than ever, I think this book is needed. People need to know that there are possibilities, and that it is time to live our passion, to find what we're good at. Even people currently in work are not invincible. That's an important fact I should bear in mind. I can remember my attitude in my last job, I thought redundancy was for others, not for me, but you never know in these times. I'm not saying this to scare you, I'm saying it to make you aware that anything is possible – good and bad – in this economy, at this moment in history, and if you're not in the job of your dreams, doing work you are passionate about, then you should realise that somebody else could do it better than you… That's the reality of things, so this is the time for you to start thinking, 'What am I good at? What can I do that others cannot do as well?' I suggest that you keep asking, go with the flow, and be open to answers. 'What am I good at? Please help me.' Put those questions out there, and stay in enquiry mode and you'll be allowing those answers to flow to you. There's no reason for you to languish under the effects of the job-search blues, or be afraid because of those figures. Yes, awful things are happening, but being fearful will not help you in your search for a dream job.

LET'S TWEET!

I came across a wonderful Twitter list: 50 Twitter Users to Follow for your Job Search. Here's the link: http://www.onedayonejob.com/blog/50-twitter-users-to-follow-for-your-job-search/. As a side note, Twitter started in 2006 and is booming now. Over four million people use it every day to send each other micro blogs, which are short updates on their status and activities. I love it. I find it friendly and fun! Check it out! And, while I'm on the subject, my Twitter account is http://twitter.com/liloumace. Let's follow each other!

This also reminded me to dust off some of the blogs I started a year ago. We had a CCOR blog, and I have a LilouMace.blogspot.com blog. I shall start posting videos and links and thoughts there.

ATTRACTING A DREAM TEAM

At the moment I am attracting my dream team, which is an interesting concept. I always used to try and do things on my own. I recognise that that is why I failed to grow my business in the USA, a business I had for seven years. Sure, I used some freelancers – many in fact – but I didn't build a team, per se. I have to say that I did not have 'a team-spirit attitude' back then.

SETTING AMBITIOUS TARGETS

I want to declare that I will have this book written in less than a month, so by mid-end March everything will have been written, and the manuscript will be ready for printing. By the 24th of April (which corresponds to the end of my Season 11) the book will be published. Wow! That's bold!

Now, those are tight deadlines, but I'm very empowered to stick to them and make it happen. I think about how energies are moving nowadays. Things are accelerating in the world, happening much faster than ever before, and in order to keep up, you have to be grounded. To be grounded you need, firstly, to have your feet firmly planted on the floor such that you are facing reality, and, secondly, you need to balance reality by developing the 'spiritual' side (for want of a better word) by such practices as visualisation, meditation and conscious application of the Law of Attraction. Without the last ones, reality can take a toll on you; it's possible to be incapacitated by fear. Conversely, if you're too 'up there', too much into visualisation, too passive, and too fearful to even get an inkling of what's happening out there, then things are not going to work for you either.

AWAKENING THE LEADER IN US

I was discussing, with my friend Laura Duksta, how much we need to step up to the mark as leaders right now – how much the world needs us. I feel I'm one of the leaders of the new revolution: an awakening of people to their power. Yes, something huge is happening; everybody is waking up. It's underway. I want to say: 'Yes, come on. Let's do it! We can do it.' The old ways of thinking are no longer useful. 'Laura,' I said, 'It's time, girl. Let's wake up. The world needs us, but it's not about us as individuals. We have our own minor issues. Let's set them aside, get our egos out of the way, and fully embrace the world's problems. Let's concentrate, and be part of this, and help others… inspire others.'

LAURA ADVISES SELF-PUBLISHING

I told Laura I was writing a book. She advised me how to get started and suggested that I self-publish. She self-published her own book, a children's book called *I Love You More*, which had its origins in a seminar. She sold 180,000 copies, and last year was able to sign a deal with a publisher in Chicago! She left me in no doubt that self-publishing was the way to go, so here we go, self-publishing all the way! She also gave me loads of useful links and advice, which I shall be following up. It's amazing, the volume of information I'm now getting! My questions are being answered along the way.

Everything is unfolding beautifully. I have updated my blog (liloumace. blogspot.com) and shall continue to post on it, and produce videos on the topic once the book is published. It's all fun!

HOPES ABOUT ERIC

I haven't heard back from Eric, the biography writer, yet. I really think he'll be the best person to put this together.

FEELING GOOD!

I just received an email from someone who just sent me a video on the subject of feeling good, the song 'Feeling Good' by Michael Buble (http://www.youtube.com/watch?v=ZSK9kkM7GL4). The lyrics could be the beginning of the book, especially when he says, 'It's a new dawn. It's a new day. It's a new life for me.' This is so much how I feel right now! What a beautiful song. I had to listen to this repeatedly!

A PROMISING CONVERSATION

Sorry… The phone is ringing…

I just had a conversation with Eric, my potential *plume*, as we say in French, and had a wonderful conversation with him. He is the one! I just know it. I can feel it. He subscribed to my video blogs on YouTube a while ago, and has been watching them over the last few months, he said, and he clearly recognises their potential. He also said the work would slot into his schedule since he's not got any pressing deadlines at the moment. Frankly, I think it would be better for me to work with Eric than with Rebecca. He has the appropriate experience. I have just sent him 30 of the first memos so that he can have a look, see if there's some potential, and see if he can improve them. He's going to give the first pages a shot, and we'll see how it comes out, but potentially I have attracted my *plume*! What's the word? 'Ghostwriter' is it? I'm not sure what the word is in English, but basically he will be editing the transcripts of my memos. It feels right.

I'm excited, yes, but, at the same time, terrified at the thought of having someone's opinion. The way I have done things feels right for me – I've just been speaking my thoughts in a simple, straightforward way – and the thought of him potentially taking it to another level is thrilling, yet I feel vulnerable. Anyway I am moving forward and then we'll talk about pricing. I told him my intention was to get it out by the end of my '100-Day Reality Challenge' season, so quite a lot needs to be done in two months. I'm super-excited!

BEING SO HAPPY THERE'S A RISK I COULD ANNOY PEOPLE

Did I say I was thankful for being fired? Oh my goodness! It's the best thing that's happened to me! I feel so alive. I want to thank my boss for having done this. I'm so happy that there's a risk it'll annoy people, but, you know what? This is the real Lilou! This is who I am, and I haven't felt like this for a long time. It feels so great and I'm so thankful. I want to give away this energy to Life, because everybody needs it right now in this time of economic hardship.

VISUALISING

I can picture myself already – visualise myself – sharing this in an interview on television shows in England, inspiring people to search for joy, to find their dream jobs and to have hope. I see myself giving hope to the entire country through such interviews, the entire world. Yes, I close my eyes, and I can see it right now. I can imagine my future. I'm living it.

You know something, the subconscious mind does not distinguish between dreams and reality, so when you close your eyes and visualise something, it could be real as far as the subconscious is concerned. Try holding an image of what you desire for at least 17 seconds. (The optimal time is something like 64 seconds – yeah, it gets quite scientific!) Live the imagined experience as vividly as you can. For example, I can picture every detail of my doing the interview I mentioned. I can also clearly see myself being interviewed by Oprah Winfrey. I can hear Oprah telling her viewers about the book and the community, calling my name, sitting on the coach next to her. Mmmm. That feels good!

COULD MY HIGH FREQUENCIES SLOW MY PROGRESS?

I just cannot get my latest video to upload onto YouTube, my iPhone is going nuts and my computer is not cooperating. Can our frequency be so high that it interferes with electronics? I am really starting to wonder. I had this problem after doing the reiki weekend. My iPhone would not stop buzzing. Now I cannot even get it to switch on. I wonder if this will become a problem on the planet if we continue to increase our energy and creative frequency? Mine have never been so high, and I am loving this, but it seems that the electronics are not!

I guess I need more powerful tools. Yeah, great excuse! I wish I could record a memo on this right now, or do a video, but I am not able to as neither of the devices is working. Groan. Glad that at least I saved the memos up until now on this computer!

I need a drink! A little glass of wine would be great right now. How can I attract a friend to go to the pub with me if I cannot even use my cell phone to reach him/her? I can only email. I could also simply go to the pub and meet someone... just go there randomly. Maybe I can simply use the power of my thoughts, think of someone friendly contacting me? Is that telepathy? I should try that stuff too. Who knows! I am always willing to try anything once!

I believe there is a reason for all this. Usually, when electronics start not to work for me it means I need a break. However, I think I am full of ideas right now and I want to get them out. Maybe I should continue this by writing them?

I wonder if at some point in the evolution of human beings we shall get to a stage where we can no longer use all these electronic devices. Maybe there will be such a clash between our high frequencies as human beings and those of electronic gadgets, the Internet, radio, etc., that there will be a collapse and we won't be able to operate them any more. This would lead us back to a pre-electronic age: no electronics, no more communication for the people that took us so far. Wow! Some cracking thoughts there. They could come out of a science fiction book, but they might not be fiction. I feel there is some truth to this, and it would be interesting to see how electronic devices – or the lack of them – will affect the evolution of us human beings.

However, 'electronic' difficulties are not going to stop me sharing my thoughts and finishing off this book and getting to the end of this quest for my dream job. I know I am pushing the Law of Attraction very far right now. I feel so aligned and so alive. My soul is so alive. It is magnificent. I even feel that my energy is so high that it might disrupt some 'conventionalities', for want of a better word – the way things have worked up to now may be overturned.

DISRUPTING THE OLD ORDER… THE REVOLUTION!

A person with new thoughts and new ways of thinking can be disruptive to the rest of the population, to organisations, to the government, and maybe even to the media. People prefer to stay in their old way of beings and to continue functioning in the ways they are used to. They see it as safer. Yet I think our planet is ready for a major change in the way we think about and do things. Our revolution has come. It is not a revolution against anyone else; it is a revolution happening within ourselves. It is time to set ourselves free from all fear, from other people's judgement, from conventional ways of thinking.

I do not think we can operate in the way we have been operating any longer. There is war, unemployment, debt, crime, and natural disasters that are so much greater than ourselves, and greater than most of us have known in our lives up until now. We just cannot operate and think the same way any more. For the sake of the world, we need to learn, to grow, to own who we truly are.

Each of us is unique. If we all fulfil our roles in society then we shall truly operate at a high level and peace can be established. We each have a unique role to play. I am different from you. I am no better. I am different. Yes, I can do some things better than you can, and you can do some things better than I can. We need each other. We need each other's help. We are brothers and sisters (as Laura Duskta would say), and if you experience problems, then those problems are also mine. We are part of one consciousness of thoughts, one big pot of ideas and thoughts. We all can tap into this infinite potential, collaborate and set ourselves free.

I hope you join me in this effort, in this revolution. It feels good and our future is bright. I was on such a natural high last night. None of those electronics wanted to cooperate so I turned them off and went out. I met my new friend Paul, and shared all my latest adventures with him. It was a nice surprise that he was able to come out on such short notice; the timing was good. It was a juicy evening – very juicy!

COMING DOWN TO PRACTICALITIES

On waking this morning I checked my YouTube account, as I diligently do every day. My videos were online and had received supportive comments. I love receiving comments! I spent some time looking at Book Surge. I discovered that they give back 35% of what you sell your book for, and there are also set-up fees, design fees, promotion fees, etc., so I started to panic a bit. This was compounded by the fact that I arranged the initial bank transfer for my new place – I have to pay two months' rent in total. To be blunt, I got scared and I am not yet ready to re-focus. I shall be doing a meditation session and a reiki on myself to recharge my batteries.

I miss my recording device. I need to find a solution to this. My iPhone is so slow right now...

I have to be gentle with myself today, and with everything around me. I did not get much sleep so I need to take it easy and re-energise so that I can then re-create something exciting for the day. I am also asking for higher guidance to see which way is the best for me. I shall get some clear answers in due course... any time now!

I also looked for a computer online, and decided that I shall be getting the beautiful iMac 24" – so inspiring! I love new toys, and, in particular, Macs, as you might have guessed. I get so creative with them.

I've just been meditating – breathing in and out calmly. It is good to feel this great energy flowing now. Despite that, I have... Oh no, I just did it again! But I am cancelling that negative thought and re-creating today as a fun, easy-going day, where things are going to work out on their own, naturally and nicely.

MONEY MANIFESTATION

My frustration with the iPhone not working isn't helping, so I need to do something about that. I might go to the Apple store after all... Yes, it is time to get the iMac! I need a splash of energy, so it is time for it 'to be manifested'. Boy, I still cannot believe sometimes how well the Law of Attraction works. Ask, and it is given. This morning £900, to be exact, came into my account from some business transaction. I never expected this money to come now! This is grand! I shall add the rest and get the iMac... maybe just the one that cost that same amount – £900. I shall see... the 24" is tempting... Loving it! Time for some shopping!

DITCH WHAT IS GETTING YOU DOWN

I was going to go to this two-day e-marketing seminar happening in London today. All the industry leaders are there, but – you know what? – I just realised that this is what has been dragging me down all morning: I just do not want to go there. I do not need to. No one is forcing me. Yes, it will be interesting, and I might pick up a new idea, but this isn't my industry any more. I am now an author, and a TV-presentation and law-of-attraction guru! Ha! I do not need to learn about email-marketing or social networks. I already know lots, and the time has come to apply my knowledge. I feel free and good again. What a relief! Something was depressing me all day. The thought of going there was daunting. There are no have-to's in life. It's time to go with a full heart to the Apple store. Yeah!

IT TAKES GUTS

In the bus on my way to the Apple store I read a few pages from the book *The Secret*. I opened the book at a point where Rhonda Byrne was explaining how each day she would say to herself how grateful she was for the movie *The Secret* and then, full of this feeling of gratitude, she let the adventures of the day unfold.

This is how I feel right now. I know what will come out of all this is extraordinary. Here I am now, without a job and focusing on the abundance of things, while my own day-to-day reality (that of the outer world) isn't there yet. Although I generally feel that at the level of my inner being I am already there, I occasionally catch myself looking at this external 'reality', and I am frightened, because a complete manifestation of my inner state isn't there, as yet. I must remain focused on my inner knowing. It takes guts to go for it, I have to say, but trust me when I say that it is worth it. Little traces of evidence tell me every day that I *am* on the right track. I feel blessed.

I wonder if I am sitting on this sofa today, without a job, because one day I said that I wanted to empower millions? Is this why I got my last job, to bring me here and then lose it? Is this the city that will wake my full potential and lead to the manifestation of my wildest dreams?

DESERVED LUXURY OR NEEDLESS EXPENSE?

I have an 8.15 p.m. appointment back at the Apple store to get my iPhone sorted. I am working on the iMac 24" right now. It is so sleek and… huge! The screen is enormous! I am starting to have doubts about it. It does not feel quite right to be working on such a big screen. I feel guilty. I think the 20" might have been enough, and I think I would feel better working on it rather than this one. Strictly speaking, I can afford this one, but my desire to manifest what I need for my work would be fully realised by the 20" one. But on the other end, these are not thoughts of abundance: I am thinking again from a 'scarcity' point of view, from a mindset of lack of money and lack of faith. I am torn. I just cannot be in this state. I feel bad, and guilty for getting into this situation. The difference between the 20" and the 24" is only £1,125 minus £785, which is £340 – not that significant when you are embarking on a major project, perhaps, but it could pay a designer.

I thought I would have felt even better with this computer and get even more inspired but I am not. The difference here might only be £340, but if this means the success of the project then I can sacrifice this, and downgrade to a 20".

A MILLION-DOLLAR IDEA LOST?

I ask for higher guidance. Please give me higher guidance! I want to be able to feel the abundance of Life right now, and know that I deserve this computer at this moment and for the project.

Wow, I cannot believe that I am spending so much of my time debating whether or not it's the right thing to do. But aren't we all like this sometimes, wasting our time on trivial decisions instead of spending time on things that matter, such as, for example, working on some brilliant ideas to sell millions of copies of my new book, to make it go viral and reach number one on Amazon and become a New York Times best-seller for weeks in a row? I could potentially have generated a crucial idea during the time I was agonising about the computer, a brilliant idea that would have made all the difference.

Maybe I am coming from a lack of abundance, but, after all, I did initially manifest the money for the 20" one. ... Interestingly, taking it back does not feel like I am giving up on the abundance of the universe; rather that I am trusting myself in what is best here. Besides, I shall then be able to get some furniture, plants and lamps... chairs to make my new place look nice, in accordance with my taste.

A QUESTION OF WHAT GETS YOU CLOSER TO YOUR NATURAL STATE OF BEING

Fundamentally it is not a question of price, but a matter of what feels good, what gets you closer to your natural state of being. A smaller and cheaper gym does not make me feel good when I go there, but a big computer screen is just not OK for me right now, so it's time to return it and get back into the 'feeling-good place'.

Did I say I love toys? Yes, toys are a big deal for me. Nothing is set in stone here. You could say that the 'test drive' didn't do it for me! Time to take it back to the shop and get my little iPhone fixed again.

OK, so I got the new iMac 20" instead of the 24". This feels really great – the right format. Now it's time for a good sleep. ...Thinking of refreshing things, a nice cleanse to start this new chapter would be great. I'll do a detox for a few days, and start soon, possibly on March 1st. Now I'm going to do some packing and to enjoy a bit of tweeting (twitter.com/liloumace). Do you tweet too? Let's connect. Off subject? OK!

THE POWER OF FREQUENT RECORDINGS

I spoke with Megan Castran from Australia (http://www.youtube.com/jewelchic), a member of CCOR and a good friend now – such an inspiration. She set my 'vibrations' to positive, as always! Her smile, *joie de vivre* and excitement are contagious.

My iPhone is also fixed now. I'm not sure which vibration mode I put it in, but when the Apple Genius Bar touched it, it was working. I had to remove the recordings and save them on my new iMac. This wasn't a problem, but I still can't record. I miss this. Frequent recording really boosts my energy levels. It keeps me very much on track, even more so then videos. Maybe I should do more frequent videos?

It's 22.47 p.m. Good night.

P.S. Tomorrow I am starting my recording. While I pack, yeah – packing and enjoying the flow of life tomorrow!

WE NEED MORE CHAMPIONS

Doesn't this economy call for inspiring champions? I mean, where is my TV gig? I'm laughing. I really think that in the present economic situation we'd benefit from some uplifting people, some champions to keep the population thinking positively about possibilities. I suppose what I'm saying is that I'm again feeling a strong sense of urgency about putting the book out, and also with regard to landing my dream job. Yes, the book and the meditation CD are very worthwhile projects, but I do not think they are ends in themselves. A TV job would be the dream job I'm looking for, yet I want to be able to hold an independent open conversation where I can really contribute, not to be stuck in a banal ratings-chasing straitjacket. The former is possibly more likely to happen over the Internet, but might well become increasingly possible on TV as more and more viewers want 'the real thing'. Anyway, I wish you a good night. It's nearly 23 minutes past midnight.

MORNING GRATITUDE AND REQUEST FOR GUIDANCE

This morning I woke up feeling grateful. I stated in my mind what I was grateful for (everything unfolding right now), and also that I wanted to be guided today, every step of the way. I'm asking Life, 'How can I find this dream job? What does it look like? How can I make a good living from my videos?'

A VISION VIDEO?

I know that being a YouTube partner can be highly profitable! The Internet definitely resonates with me. Appearing on the Internet, as part of a network, a well-known network, would be awesome. My dream job would involve interviewing the authors of self-help books in a TV studio, at home, or over the web, but it would require the help of a team and various resources, and I would want to earn a great income from it. That sounds good and feels great. Perhaps I should start putting together a little digital vision board with images of the team, the network, the cameras, the people interacting, etc. Yes, I'm going to work on that and it'll also a good way of familiarising myself with the iMovie09 which I haven't used yet, although I used to use iMovie on the old Macs, which was very simple.

CATCHING AND DESPATCHING A NEGATIVE THOUGHT

I caught myself thinking there that the new software is going to be much more complicated! I have to shift my way of thinking, because if I believe it's going to be complicated then I know I'm going to make things complicated for no good reason. So now I'm telling myself that I'm going to figure it out very easily, and it will be a great experience, and that the movie will be out in no time, and I'll share it on YouTube. I feel it's going to be a very worthwhile exercise. I am looking forward to doing it, and to trying it with you!

WHEN LESS IS BETTER

I really love the notion of doing fewer things and visualising more, and then, as a result, actually achieving more! I think I'm one of those people whose life tends to consist of rush, rush, rush, do, do, do – keeping busy all the time. I am learning to prioritise, to do the things that matter the most, but do I take enough time to visualise, to get clear on my vision? I think that stage of the creative process is the part that should take the longest, or should receive the most attention. I'm now starting on my vision video. I'm going to Google. com and then once in there, I'm going to click on the left-hand corner, on 'Images' (there's also Web, Map, News, etc.). Once I'm on Google Image Search I'm going to type in some keywords such as 'television'. How about 'television crew'? – it's all about the crew – 'television crew', and here we are. I have thousands to choose from. I'm just going to take those that feel right. For some reason, I like the BBC and so I just entered, instead of just 'television crew', 'BBC TV television crew'. I've also picked up the BBC logo and I'm continuing to look.

You have to choose those images carefully because, as we know, those things truly happen, and you're going to spend some time looking at them and being with the feelings they generate. If an image makes you feel stressed or uncomfortable, therefore, or simply doesn't generate a good feeling, then don't use it. Through looking at all this, I'm now thinking do I actually want to have a crew? So the process helps me define what I want, what feels right, what resonates.

FLIPPING TO MILLIONS

I've also found an image showing a YouTube video that has had 33 million views, so I'm going to incorporate that to illustrate high traffic: Internet popularity! Also, I'm a big fan of the Flip camera (www. theflip.com) so I'm going to add a picture of one of those. I already have one, but I would love the HD Flip camera, and, even more than that, I would love to have sponsors like Flip approach me and say, 'We want you to represent our brand.' Because making videos is something I do anyway, it would be great to be able to promote the relevant brands I believe in, and receive, in return, new products, commissions on sales through my sites, sponsorship, or a salary.

CREATED FROM A THOUGHT

Now, I've typed 'TV interviews', but it's not delivering the feeling I'm looking for. They all look too formal. It's not quite my style, so I have to expand my search, possibly to include webcam interviews, and maybe travel interviews because I'd love to interview people with an exotic location – spectacular scenery – in the background! I can imagine a show that mixes travel and inspiration. Yes, I would love to attract that, to attract a tailor-made TV show, one that would satisfy my thirst for travel and wisdom at the same time. I can imagine a TV producer picking up on my ideas and saying something like, 'Yeah, there's something to be made there, you know, and she's the perfect person to front it. We'll create the show around that concept.' Now, I'm not saying all this in an arrogant way, I hope – ha, ha! I'm just illustrating how you can arrive at something that fully attracts you… that's so well suited to you. This show I've just imagined can be created, from nothing…well from a thought! Yes, our thoughts are that powerful. It doesn't have to exist right now. I have to keep an open mind in that regard.

TRAVELLING FIRST-CLASS ON VIRGIN ATLANTIC

Strangely, I still haven't found my travel interview image, but I've stumbled on a picture of a plane. Now, I love planes. The thought of them gets me really excited, so now I've entered 'First Class Virgin'. I would love to travel in first class, and I really like Virgin as a brand. I think Richard Branson is an amazing leader, very inspiring. I'm reading his book at the moment – *Business Stripped Bare*. But how about a picture of the first-class cabin of a Virgin Atlantic plane? I like that idea, so I'm going to pick it. I can see myself with a glass of champagne and some friends, enjoying the luxury of the trans-Atlantic flight in first class on my way to Hawaii! I have never been first-class, but could imagine getting used to it! My imagination is at work! 'Lovely!' as the Brits would say.

THE MOUNTAIN TOP

Now, I'm imagining breathtaking views from a mountain top. I feel a strong connection with this, so I'm looking for various inspiring images of this nature. There's such a symbolism to a mountain peak. I've had this really clear image in my mind for quite some time.

Now I'm looking at the images I've found by searching for 'mountain top'. I've come across this absolutely magnificent picture. It's a sunset scene, seen from above the clouds, and there's a little mountain peak just appearing above them. It's stunning. There's another one showing this person with her arms wide, on top of a mountain, so there's a lot of symbolism there too: freedom and this surreal, beautiful closeness to God and creation. I'm bringing the word 'God' into things now, but I don't often mention it and used to mention it even less often, but the more I get into this work, the more connected I feel with 'the source', with the Universe, to Life. For me it's like a powerful form of energy that is beyond the mind, yet intertwined with it. It's a divine feeling of creative power and of oneness. That's how I feel when I see that mountain top. It's as if my soul is light, and perfectly aligned. That's the place of feeling good that you constantly strive to reach. That's the feeling you are seeking to create when you choose your pictures. My worries disappear.

ADVICE FROM 'RICH DAD, POOR DAD'

This is a little memo on the side. I have to share something with you. PhilosophersNotes.com is an amazing little website. I'm going to listen to the summary of *Rich Dad, Poor Dad*, which I've downloaded from the website. It's a book I've never read but heard great things about. So how long will it take me? Eighteen minutes, 17 seconds – that's all! I can definitely find time for that. How about listening to it while packing for my move? How fabulous! Two in one.

WHAT WOULD YOU DO IF YOU KNEW YOU WOULD SUCCEED?

What I'm getting out of listening to the summary of Robert Kiyosaki's *Rich Dad, Poor Dad* is that the question of fundamental importance is: 'What would you do right now if you were not afraid, and if you were guaranteed to succeed in whatever you chose to do with your life?'

Take a moment now to think about that, and write your answer here or in your journal. What would you do if you could do anything? This is where I'm coming from with the whole passion and dreams thing. This is why the creation of a vision video (or vision board) is really helpful, because it will help you to start dreaming. You must put yourself in that place where anything is possible, and then things start to flow. It's interesting to think about this. What would you do if you could do anything that you wanted to, and you knew you would succeed at it? What would it look like?

REACTING TO CHALLENGES

Robert Kiyosaki, as summarised by Brian Johnson, then goes on to talk about the importance of your reaction to failure. It's your response to such circumstances that is crucial, and, as you can see from everything that's been happening to me so far, that is, to a large extent, what this book is about. Your attitude can totally shift everything in your life. It's not too late. *Knowing.*

Some people will be inventing things, starting new businesses, and new partnerships, and many may prosper. Amazing ideas are created during times of crisis. This is a time to re-invent ourselves. But this can only be done if we see everything happening right now as an opportunity.

Stand up with me and declare: 'I am so grateful that I have now attracted my dream job. Thank you for this blessing.' Say this affirmation every day when you wake up in the morning. You know, the United States were not yet independent from the British when the Declaration of Independence was written. Declarations are that powerful!

WE HAVE A NEW JOB!

You know what our new job actually is? Our job is to find what we want. Yes! This is our new job!

TEN LITTLE GRATITUDE STONES

About a month ago I visited friends in Mougins-le-Haut, not far from Cannes in the south of France. What a beautiful area – *magnifique*! I loved it, despite the fact that the weather conditions put paid to our plans to go skiing. We ended up simply walking along the sea front – Isabelle, Christophe, their newborn baby, little Marine, and myself.

It was a very relaxing time, but some worries about my job bubbled to the surface so I took the opportunity to update my resumé.

I picked up some pebbles, which I call 'gratitude stones', as do many of us who consciously and deliberately apply the Law of Attraction. The idea is that you keep one in your car, in your wallet, or at home, and then every time you see it, it reminds you to be grateful for something in your life. I collected ten of them, and I remember saying to myself, 'You know what? I'm taking those ten little gratitude rocks, and somehow, some day, I will find some people who can use them.'

I picked up my own one in the Zion National Park in Utah, while I was hiking with my mom preparing for the Rock'n'Roll Half Marathon we did together two years ago in Phoenix, Arizona. We had lived in Arizona over 20 years ago, from when I was six until I was eight, so this was a way for us to spend some quality time, visit Scottsdale again and have a good workout!

I had picked up those ten little stones for people unknown, and it's weird, because now that I'm packing my things I have come across them again, and now I think, 'Of course, I know who those little rocks were supposed to be for – the ten boys who are taking part in the project in Brixton, in the south of London. How perfect!' Seeing those pebbles now, takes me straight back to the beach – I remember vividly my strange certainty that there was a reason for collecting them.

This episode is a little inspiration in itself – another sign to tell me that I am on the right track ...and if you don't have a gratitude stone then it's also a suggestion for you! Pebbles, rocks and stones are a fascinating topic in themselves. Many have such beautiful shapes. I find them rather like mountains and trees in their power to inspire. I don't know if you've been around big mountains, but their aura of ancient permanence gives me a feeling of grounding, as does the little pebble I carry. It feels as if I give it more energy every time I touch it, so it's a very powerful little rock by now.

It makes me so happy to know to whom those other ten are going!

EXPERIMENT WITH VISUALISING YOUR GOALS

I'm just reading a comment someone has posted in response to one of my videos:

I just think that no matter how vivid my visualisations are, I'm almost sure the universe will not bring about the opportunity for them to be fulfilled.

Well, guess what, buddy? That's what you're going to get. Our task is not just to sit there, and visualise, and do nothing apart from try to think that what we want is going to come to us. Our task is to align ourselves with the feeling – the knowledge – that we deserve it, and bask in the fact that it feels good. If it doesn't feel good, then maybe that's not it for you. Start exploring other things. Try different possibilities. Experiment the way Edison would do, as was explained to me by Sarah Caldicott, his great grandniece, whom I interviewed on *My Juicy Life* back in Chicago.

I loved interviewing those authors of self-help books! Sarah had some very interesting things to say, not least about how playful Edison was. (See 'Edison loved the journey!': http://www.youtube. com/watch?v=lktDPlh8hlE) I mean the guy eventually invented the light bulb, but only after hundreds of experiments, so he had to enjoy the process to keep going. A good way to adopt the right attitude to your life would be to think about trying different approaches as you might try on different clothes – try something else, a new style. I know change can sometimes be scary, but just 'try it on' and test it with whatever you choose to visualise. How do your mental pictures make you feel? The more you practise, the easier it gets! Practice makes perfect!

HAVE FUN!

At some point I can see myself in a big studio with lots of cameras and a big audience. I wouldn't mind being interviewed in such fine circumstances, but being the interviewer and having my own show is not where I'm at right now; it doesn't feel right. It's not exactly what I want to attract, but, on the other hand, being out there, being connected with the world, through YouTube and travel, and having supportive and talented people around me... Yes, there's something about that that feels right, and so it's just a matter of fine-tuning, experimenting, experimenting, and experimenting again, to try out various scenarios, and having fun with them! Do this yourself now. Play with images. Play with your mind. Enjoy the process. Stop being so serious!

By the way, you might be interested in my Vision Video, which will give you an idea of how my ideas have evolved since I made it in July 2007: http://www.youtube.com/watch?v=DpdE0ahRnak. It's had about 12,000 hits.

YOUR INTUITION KICKS IN WHEN YOU'RE IN THE FLOW

I recently posted a video about the difference between the Law of Attraction and Positivity (http://www.youtube.com/watch?v=FZZ5Ubj3uW0), concepts I think many people confuse. One of the commentators on this video says, 'Oh, some time ago you interviewed Sonia Choquette. Why don't you give her a call for insight, info, and encouragement? Keep going strong.' (The video of this interview was titled 'What is intuition and how you can develop it' and you may view it here: http://www.youtube.com/watch?v=QiX3VVeaPbE .) Yes, paradiseonearthNL, Sonia Choquette is a wonderful person. I really enjoyed meeting her, and she wrote amazing books, one of which I bought (*Trust Your Vibes*). She's an expert on intuition and, yes, giving her a call might seem like a good idea, but, you know what? I think that when you practise the Law of Attraction and succeed in getting into the flow, where I am now, then your own intuition and feelings about things become clearer and stronger. I agree!

ANGEL CARDS TAUGHT ME TO USE MY INTUITION

Using cards, by the way, is certainly a tool that helped me. Thinking of Angel cards, for example, some years ago I used them, and, whatever you may think about the wackiness of it, they really did help. I would draw a card from the pack and it might say something like, 'Eat healthily.' or 'Spend some time in nature.' or 'Follow your inner guidance.' Those are just some examples. Although I was supposedly asking angels for answers I was really asking myself, because, of course, it was me interpreting the cards. This gave me an opportunity, then, to start building up that 'intuition muscle' and, ultimately, it led me to a raw food diet.

A HEALTHY DIET LEADS TO AN INTUITIVE BODY AND MIND

I did the Master Cleanse, which I shall explain later, and from there I started eating raw food. I love eating healthy food now. What does that this have to do with intuition? Well, the healthier your body, the more intuitive you get – the better you nourish yourself, the better your intuition becomes. It's as if a cloud lifts and you think clearly, and things flow and seem natural…

There are also other exercises you can use to develop your intuition. Simply asking yourself for some answers, or asking for higher guidance, will produce results. The guidance or answers may appear inside you, or outside in the physical world, but, whatever forms they may take, it's up to you, the individual, to do the interpretation.

I'm not, therefore, going to call Sonia Choquette for her recommendations right now. I would love, however, to interview her again at some point. Now doesn't feel like the right time; I'll almost certainly meet her again. For now I'm simply tapping into my own intuitive guidance, and following it step by step, as I'm creating – as I'm asking, it is given.

THE LAW OF ATTRACTION AS A PERFECT MANAGER

I saw a wonderful Jerry and Esther Hicks video yesterday on YouTube. It explained that the Law of Attraction can be thought of as a perfect manager, someone you can ask for anything that you want, such as: 'I would like more money.' or 'Please, I would like the team that I need to put this project in place.' or 'I want to prosper.' Ask in that way, if you want, as if you are addressing a person rather than the impersonal Universe. I also love the 'placemat' technique and the '100-dollar bill in your wallet' trick. But that is for another time!

BIG OR SMALL, LIFE DOES NOT MAKE THE DISTINCTION IF YOU DON'T!

Ask your questions – put them out there, no excuses, no doubts or guilt for asking. Just affirm them – and things will unfold. I promise you things will unfold, and the more you practise, the quicker it gets. When you initially try to manifest things it might take three months, six months, or a year, depending on how big the thing you want to manifest is, but if you build your confidence by starting with small things it will snowball: you will manifest increasingly more, increasingly quickly. With me it's only a matter of days most of the time now, depending on how big the thing I want to manifest, so it's pretty awesome!

I am reminding myself that Life does not make the distinction between big and small. It is our perceptions that shape things, our thoughts that we put out that 'this should take time, and this won't' that will increase or decrease the speed at which things will manifest.

A NEW VISION VIDEO

I'm working on a new vision 'board', one I'm creating on my computer in the form of a video. I am selecting images to include in it. Ones that make me feel great, that are 100% right and of which I'm totally sure.

I'm finished now; it was very quick to do. I'm going to have a beautiful last lunch in this area, which I shall soon be leaving. I'll walk around and take some time to say goodbye, and enjoy the experience.

THE FITNESS CAFÉ: IT SHOWS WHEN YOU DO WHAT YOU LOVE

I'm just back from wandering around my neighbourhood. I ended up having lunch at The Fitness Café, just off Abbey Road. There is such a feeling of abundance that resides in it... so full of life, and the food was so good and fresh, and there were so many marvellous details in the décor. You can tell that the people who run it love it, and are passionate about health and wellbeing. That shop radiates fitness!

There's so much to be said for living your dream like that. It's so attractive to see people who are really on purpose. They are so creative and contagiously inspiring. They go out of their way to serve you well and make you feel welcome. The experience is awesome – you can feel the love there. That was really great, and it makes me think again that in the competitive marketplace we have today, if we don't do something that we love, it's unlikely that we will be good enough. I think that only people who love what they're doing will succeed: people who take things beyond the merely 'acceptable', and are truly creative and resourceful.

MY LAST JOB WAS INCOMPATIBLE WITH MY MISSION STATEMENT

It's 3.11 – another 11! I'm looking at my own website (http://www. LilouMace.com) as I wanted to grab a picture of myself for my vision video. I just took a moment to read my personal mission statement on the home page. For now it says:

1. *To inspire, motivate, and empower millions of people to pursue their dreams.*

2. *To help spread joy, freedom, and empowerment.*

3. *To demonstrate that anything is possible.*

4. *To work with integrity and passion at all times.*

5. *To encourage and fund thousands of children to travel to foreign countries.*

6. *To remain humble and grateful no matter what success comes my way.*

7. *To transform the self-development industry.*

8. *To give away and freely my energy and joy to people on this journey.*

9. *To love, give, and share more each day.*

10. *To apply daily Universal laws and principles.*

Looking at this, it's obvious that my last job was unsuitable. I could not even say that one of the points seemed real and tangible. Now, I feel that all of them are coming alive, as I speak this book and imagine the shape my dream will take to fulfil them. I've long been stating my mission, as expressed on the website. No wonder I felt bad in my job. No wonder my inner Self was aware of something missing. My work just wasn't resonating with my declaration, with what I really wanted, which is what I've just stated and which is right in front of me now – even though I wrote it years ago. I've got to keep that personal mission statement in the forefront of my awareness. I recommend that you also create one. It's really powerful. I should perhaps write it down and read it every day. I also want to prepare a declaration, of half a page or a page, on how I see life, and how things are working out and manifesting.

AN ORGANIC PROCESS

Following the Law of Attraction is an organic and flexible process, not a rigorously plotted and scheduled one. The right advice or input arrives naturally when you're in the flow.

I've met people. I've received emails. I share their work, and this just naturally unfolds. We're here to help each other, and I help others, but I don't do this with an agenda in mind. I allow Life to bring the various elements that I need to fulfil my intentions.

A NEW GENERATION OF LEADERSHIP

I feel there is a new type of leadership. The new generation's style of leadership is emerging, where leaders are part of the communities they influence and they live the same problems – they do not pretend to have everything sorted. We are all in the same boat. We all experience difficulties. I do not think you gain more authority as a leader by sharing only your success stories, saying, 'I have done this and that, and this is the way to go'. People seem to be more inspired by watching someone experiencing the same challenges and setbacks at the same time. Internet video allows this; books allow this, and I love it. I am so grateful for these outlets. I hope to be part of this new-leadership revolution, if I can call it that, and to see how it unfolds.

DECLARATIONS

Here's a little declaration I put together. It took me 20 minutes. It's only half a page on my computer screen – a few paragraphs. Declarations don't have to take time. They don't have to be long. I've done a similar one before, but this one feels right just now.

Lilou's Declaration:

I live in the context that anything is possible, through declaring it, claiming it, and visualising it. I declare that I inspire, motivate, and empower millions of people daily to pursue their dreams. I help spread joy, freedom, and empowerment on the planet. My life is juicy, and things work out magically and abundantly. I demonstrate that anything is possible. Daily I apply Universal laws and principles, and give away my energy and joy to millions along this journey. I work with integrity and passion at all times. I love, give, and share more each day, and I feel grateful every day for my life.

I declare that my energy, enthusiasm, determination, passion, wisdom, creativity and love inspire a visionary and talented television producer and TV network to choose me as their new TV host. This show is fun, educational, entertaining, hip. Millions of viewers of all ages and all backgrounds are empowered to live life to the fullest: A Juicy Life! My interviews, travel, and passion for this work shine out, and people tune in diligently to watch all new episodes. This is a real success on all level. I transform the self-development industry, and follow my passion for wanting to make a difference.

My book series is a real success, and all my books are New York Times bestsellers. The first book is magnetic, and millions of people buy it for themselves, their friends, and families, to show their support. It is an act of love. I am so thankful for all the wonderful people I met that helped me, and that wanted to make this project possible.

I start a 'One-World, One-Travel' foundation, and thousands of kids around the world take a plane for the first time, and see new cultures. It transforms their lives forever. They start to dream big. They share the magic around them, and are champions in their lives.

I, Lilou Mace, declare myself to be a magnificent leader and champion for people. I lead a new type of revolution. This revolution opens people up to their dreams, and what is possible. My declarations and dream are fulfilled.

Now, as you can see, this declaration is not very long, but by producing such a declaration, and reading it every day, you can acquire an increasingly deeper sense of purpose.

write it

I recommend you start writing your declaration in your journal now. Jot down a first draft, and then type it up. Once it's typed, you can tweak it – change words here and there – and then before you know it, you'll have something that resonates with your inner Self very powerfully. It's best to keep it short, and it should state things that you feel very strongly about – about which you have no doubts. I used to have one that was four pages long, and you can hear me read it in this video: http://www.youtube.com/watch?v=rkTD0BcTPuI. I don't know where I've put the written version now. The one I've just created is a bit shorter so I can read it daily and focus ever more effectively on what's possible in my life.

I've been carrying a mini-declaration in my wallet too. I wrote it on a piece of paper a few months ago. It is only a few lines but each time I see it, I read it, wherever I am. It's another little reinforcement you might want to try.

CARD

I also have a card in there that says: 'My mission is to help millions of people to live a life of passion and purpose, a juicy life.' I often look at this one too. It's laminated and was made by Sandy (http://www. cocreatingourreality.com/profile/Sandy65), one of the UK members of the 'Co-Creating Our Reality' community. It reminds me to live a juicy life!

VISION VIDEO FINISHED

see it

OK, so I've finished my 'Lilou's Vision Video' (http://www. cocreatingourreality.com/video/lilous-vision-video). It shows various chapters of my life. Oprah's in there and there is a bit about being a New York Times best-selling author and several other things. It's not quite in sequence – I struggled a bit with that aspect – but it's fun. I think it's two minutes and 20 seconds, and I've used various picture transition options and added text and music. It's a playful little vision video for March '09, which I'm going to watch as often as I can – daily!

Yes, I will brainwash myself until the point where I can feel it as if it as real, and have no doubts that this is happening and taking place!

Warning: Be careful what you wish for! This stuff works, you know! I have put it to the test many times!

A LAW-OF-ATTRACTION STORY: THE BRIDE TOOK SIX MONTHS TO SHOW UP!

This is my last night in St. John's Wood, and I'm walking along Abbey Road. I just had a great dinner with my dear friend Nami, whom I met shortly after I arrived here. She just told me this amazing story about her twin brother going back to India and meeting a childhood friend of hers at their cousin's wedding. Within two days he just knew he wanted to marry her – they were engaged within a week. They're both 37 and getting married soon. I found that amazing. It's a fabulous little Law-of-Attraction story considering that six months ago he had declared: 'I will meet the right woman, and be married within six months.' A beautiful story!

MOVING TO EARL'S COURT, AND CANCELLING NEGATIVE THOUGHTS

Today, I'm moving to my new home in Earl's Court. I'm really excited, although, because of the stress of preparation and everything that is happening today, I have the occasional negative thought. Every time one springs up I cancel it, and re-create from there. It's just a matter of practice and being aware of it when these arise and dealing with them promptly, otherwise they would rush in, one after the other, and before I'd know it I'd have a bad day, as might happen if you, say, stubbed a toe after getting out of bed, or spilt something on your freshly laundered skirt… It's more or less the same here. You have to consciously call a halt to the negativity, or it can spiral out of control. I'm creating the possibility, then, of having a delightful, smooth, fun day, during which things are going to work perfectly. And then… Yeah, the other idea that I have… Oops, a negative thought! I'll just cancel it, and re-create something else, something more fun and more positive.

Boy, it's 11.11. Oh my goodness! This must mean that I'm really on track: every time I see the clock (often) it says something-11: 3.11, 4.11. Now 11.11. I feel so good!

MEETING JUSTIN

I moved into my new house in Earl's Court yesterday. The move went well – pretty smoothly. Funnily enough, I was helped by Justin, who is moving in with my previous flatmate, and who is also going through a transitional period. He just broke up with his girlfriend and is starting anew, so we spent the day together – we helped each other with the physical business of the move, but also emotionally. I shall probably never see him again, but it was one of those moments when you share a bit of your life with someone and it feels as if there's a reason for it. There were so many parallels between our stories – starting something new and moving – and it was really interesting. I'd like to think that it helped both of us get complete and turn the page on our past to start afresh.

CREATIVITY

Anyway, the move went really well, and after that I settled in. I bought some new furniture with a kind of Zen feel to it, and a little bonsai tree, and I arranged these in my big room, giving it a really nurturing and creative atmosphere. (By the way, I share this big flat with Henrik, a Danish IT genius, and Giada, a sophisticated, arty 27-year-old Italian.) Anyway, after setting up my room I had a good sleep, as you can imagine, and then this morning I woke up to discover that I had received the books I'd ordered from Amazon. They are *The*

Artist's Way, the *Petit Cahier d'Exercices du Lâcher-Prise* and the *Petit Cahier d'Exercices d'Estime de Soi* ('The Little Exercise Book of Letting Go' and 'The Little Exercise Book of Self-Esteem'), which I'm going to review. The great thing, though, is that I read a few pages of *The Artist's Way*, on how you can tap into your creative power, and that's exactly what I feel has been happening with me since the beginning of this whole journey. Oops! I was going towards Earl's Court station but I've gone the wrong way so I'm going to walk a little bit more...

THE BOOK IS BECOMING REAL!

By the way, I've found this is the best way to record my memos – when I'm walking outdoors – because I don't want to disturb my new housemates.

I read my editor's email, and I was really moved by it. It's exactly what I've been looking for; it was amazing! He did rewrite my memos, but kept them very close to what I wanted, just improving the grammar and changing a word here and there, but the energy remains. I was just so moved. We've also added headings to each memo to keep the story clear and signpost its progression; he felt that was needed.

Anyway, I think it is brilliant. I haven't absolutely decided on the title yet, but it's really exciting, it's definitely coming together, and when I read the blurb he did... Yes, he also did a blurb for me to show me what his skills are, and I was moved to tears, thinking, 'Man, this is coming together. This is becoming real now!' In that instant I could picture the end product, and the impact the book will have. I was so moved and thankful to have attracted Eric into my life to help me write this book!

MASCHA ADDS MOMENTUM, AND A BOOK LAUNCH / CCOR EXTRAVAGANZA TAKES SHAPE

After that I received an email from Mascha in Holland, one of the first members of the Co-Creator community and one of the first participants in the '100-Day Reality Challenge' (http://www.cocreatingourreality. com/profile/Mascha). She's an absolute angel – Mascha, you're an angel! …With her blonde hair – very blonde! – and blue Dutch eyes. Anyway, she was asking if we could meet on the weekend of 24 April, and I started replying to her email: 'Yeah, I would love to meet you. There couldn't be any better way for me to finish Season 11. I feel as if I've known you forever, yet we've never met.'

I am so excited how all this is unfolding, because, as I was writing this reply, agreeing that we should meet, I thought that perhaps we should also meet other CCOR participants. That sounded good! And then, before I knew it, I was drawing up a schedule for the entire weekend for all of us to meet and visit some places of interest in London. This would include a meditation session in a park, and a trip to the theatre.

I could even launch the book in London that weekend. I could give away my book to participants. Yes, I could invite them from all over the world to come to London, and meet, and discuss the book, and share ideas. How great that would be!

HIJACKING THE IDEAS FOR SINGLES' EVENTS FOR SOMETHING BIGGER

So I've just sent Mascha an email outlining my ideas, and I can't wait to hear back from her. I'm sure she's going to be super-excited. Of course I outlined to her the little programme I'd devised, complete with meditations and all kinds of things. I think we could easily get 30 or 50 people to come over – at least 30! – and we can organise dinners… and it's all coming together!   The funniest aspect of this is that because I wanted to organise those singles' events (the dinner and the getaway), all the elements are already there. Instead of doing it for singles I just do it for 'Co-Creating Our Reality'.

So it's all systems go, and I feel powerfully impelled to proceed. Everything is working out! It's amazing, and so today, I'm going to settle in my new place, but I can't wait to hear back from Mascha and from Eric, so that we can really get this going.

CELEBRATORY VEUVE CLIQUOT, AND THOUGHTS OF DANIEL

I just got a bottle of yellow label Veuve Cliquot Champagne – one of my favourites. It's a favourite because it reminds me of my best friend over in Florida, Daniel. I remember our trips in Florida in the limousine and the fun we had there. Daniel is a soul mate. I love him to pieces. I have learned so much from him; we had so many great conversations that both of us needed at the time. He's such a beautiful, amazing human being. But, anyway, I thought of you, Daniel, and I'm celebrating this with you because today there's a lot to celebrate, so Veuve Cliquot is the right one! It is as if you were here with me to celebrate today, to celebrate this beautiful happening: the book coming out, and all of it coming together.

Celebrate right now for the coming success: vibrating at that intensity now is a key part of the Law of Attraction! Being grateful for what is about to happen is celebration! It's happening. So much to celebrate right now, to enjoy, while still being responsible: just a little glass of bubbly, with some lovely freshly made hummus from my flatmate, and smoked salmon, and some Danish bread with a little glass of Mimosa (that is champagne with fresh orange juice – great for brunch!)

MY CHOICE TO BE A RAW VEGAN

I know this isn't very raw vegan, and I have to admit that I've lapsed over the last few days. What I'm going to do very soon – probably in the next few days – is start a Master Cleanse again, to clean my body so that I don't have those cravings. Having said that, I do eat pretty healthily anyway; I was brought up by my mom to eat that way. I just love healthy foods, but this has been a bit of a treat, the past few days, and it's fine. I'll get back to the raw vegan diet. That's all for now.

I still love bread, butter and cheese. I am French after all! But I choose to live a raw vegan way of life for health reasons, to have constant energy throughout the day, and keep my weight down. I am also concerned about processed foods and the quality of the food that restaurants use. I have to add that if my body craves something like fish or yoghurt, for instance, I will have it. My body is my guide and tells me what it needs, not from a place of addiction but from one of real need.

FENG SHUI

My new room faces north. I'm going to feng shui it – as I like to say (pronounced 'fung-shway'). Each part of your home corresponds to an aspect of your life. I think it's a fantastic way to harmonize the home and harmonize the flow of energies. It's funny, you can see what's going wrong with someone's life by looking at their home environment: you might find, for instance, that the areas corresponding to troubled aspects of their lives are full of clutter. Feng shui is a 4,000-year-old Japanese technique. It gets very complex, but I practise a simplified version of it. The significance of an area depends on its orientation to the main entrance. For example, south, in my flat, corresponds to fame and reputation. There is an area that represents travel, there's one for friends, another for health, and one for money. For each of these there are things you can alter to improve your life.

All right, so on with the feng shui of my new place now! Well, I will only do it for my room for now as I am sharing this flat. You start by dividing the floor plan of your home into nine sections or zones, known as 'guas'. If you're curious about this, just search the Internet for 'feng shui map', or visit the site I'm using now: www.fengshuipalace.com.

Fame and Reputation

I'm starting with the area of my room representing reputation and fame. According to the website, you need to use the colour red, and objects that reflect how you want to be seen by others. It's also good to place wooden objects in this section and add some candles. Let this area shine!

Relationships

Now, I'm going into the relationship (marriage and friendship) gua. Wow! I should pay particular attention to this one! I am single! So, for this area of the home, it's good to put things in pairs and have some objects or pictures that represent relationships or union. Instinctively, I had put the picture of the wedding of one of my best friends there. For me Isabelle and Christophe represent true love, and are a great example to me of what is possible. I'll put some paired objects there too. I've also added some photographs of good friends, including good friends of my mother, people who have known me since I was born and who were customers at the restaurant my parents used to have in Santa Barbara, California. Yes, Nina and Marcel are there – a wonderful, beautiful couple, and a great example of growing old together, and abundant, lasting love and devotion. Representing my own friendships there's a picture of Cécile and me. I've also put two pillows on my little seat in that gua, and placed two red candles there since the colour red and pink are recommended in this gua. That's all I can think of that I have that might be suitable.

Creativity

Now, I'm going to start looking at the creativity gua, which is above my chimney at the eastern side of my room. So I am adding some books to develop my creativity. I am also adding some unusual object that strike me as being creative, as well as a painting from one of my flatmate's friends. It looks good here. I am also being creative by using the empty bottle of Veuve Cliquot. I'm popping a candle in it and placing it on the chimney. This is fun!

Travel and helpful people

This corresponds to the north-west of my room. The website says: '…you find the right people in front of you at exactly the right time. Maybe it's someone you know, or perhaps it's [somebody that comes and] help[s you] out of the blue'. This all sounds good. So I am going to add my little 'circle of friends' statue, as well as some pictures of great friends, and of my mom, as well as my reiki diploma. I am also planning to put in this section my angel cards, photo album and travel books (relating to places I would like to visit, such as Thailand and Costa Rica).

Now I'm having a little break before I finish the feng shui, and eating a wonderful avocado. Did I say I love avocados? They're so good for us. I simply added a little pinch of Himalayan salt and some parsley and *voilà*! This is yum!

Career and life path

Now, I'm at the career/life path gua, which is north for me. This is where I have my desk. The website says you should pay particular attention to this gua if you want if you want to make more money in business or if you want a job, a new job, or to figure out what you are supposed to be doing in life. Excellent! Exactly what I need!

Well, well, well... Let me have a close look at this area! It says to have water here – vases and aquariums, for instance. It's apparently very important to place objects here that might denote a new direction and job. This should be done consciously and with intention – adding such an intention makes it work faster. OK, this makes sense!

My desk happens to be in my career area. The best element is water and another good element choice is metal. The best colour is black. This is perfect! My desk is metal. I have my computer, which has a lot of metal in it. I definitely have black: the printer and the lamp. It's working well! I also have some plants, which, for me, represent water. I'm going to fetch the flowers that I put over in my creative area and put it here on this table. I just tossed some old seashells in the bin, but I'm going to retrieve them and put them in this career gua. What else? I have to find some more metal. I have many metal objects, actually, and many of them are already here, so it seems like I'm doing pretty well already, but I'm going to check whether there are some more things I can use to rebalance this area.

Generally speaking I was doing pretty well in that area! YES! I'm definitely on my way – and living my dream job right now – so I'm not too surprised.

Knowledge

Now the knowledge area – that's the north-east for me. I have placed a big mirror on the right-hand side of my desk, because when I'm sitting at my desk (in the northern part of the room) my back is towards the door. I've heard that in situations like this you should place a mirror in front or to the side so that you can see from this place who is walking in, otherwise others will supposedly tend to stab you in the back or talk behind it. I am also adding some cushions and candles as they say that this is a great place for meditation. And finally I am putting my bonsai tree there too, on the right of my desk, which is in the knowledge gua.

Family and foundation

OK, now this is challenging because this corresponds to my cupboard and bed area, so I might have to put something on top of the cupboard up there that would represent lineage. The only thing I can think of adding is my beautiful white stone cross, which has a fish engraved on it. I bought it on Sanibel Island a few years ago. It represents God for me. I think this is a great spot to put it.

Prosperity and abundance

So the final part I have to feng shui is the prosperity/abundance gua. This is the south-east corner of my room, and I have a cupboard there of which the contents are not exactly tidy, even though I just moved in, so I definitely have to work on that!

I need to figure out how to do this, because I have a lot of mess in there: hats, gloves, bags and all kinds of things. Anyway, apparently the best colour choice is purple; other good colours are red, green, and gold, and good element choices are wood and water. OK, so I am going to clean up my cupboard, add a little table there, and put my red jewellery box on it, and as well as add my pictures with Oprah Winfrey. I am also placing *The Science of Getting Rich*, *The Four Spiritual Laws of Prosperity* and my favourite, *The Little Money Bible*, on this table also.

Yeahhhhhhh! I am done. ☺

HOW WILL THE BOOK END? WHAT WILL I DO NEXT?

I'm outdoors now. The room is beautiful, harmonious, and feels just great. This has given me the sense of tackling every single area of my life, making sure that it all works, and setting myself up to win, to make it all happen, so now I want to declare that – imagine a drum rolling now! – it is time to manifest something big, something to end this book! I need something to wrap this story up. I am living the dream. I am writing this book, and everything is falling into place, including a CCOR event that I'm going to put together. As far as the book goes, this is all building nicely too: the editor and the designer are in place. Of course, there are still some things to tie up there, but I declare it will be launched on April 24. Yes, that is now the date by which it will be available on Amazon and printed etc. So now it's a matter of...? I'm not sure!

I just don't know how this story is going to end, how this book is going to end. The book will have to end, but, come to think of it, the story could go on forever. Yes, there will be a continuation. I'm a job seeker, looking for my dream job. What would the ideal outcome be? I don't know. If I were to find a publisher, then I guess it would be that, but right now I'm not yet sure, so I'm asking for higher guidance. I'm asking for help, and we'll see.

For now, I have arranged to interview Brian Johnson on his *PhilosophersNotes*. It'll be one of my little five-minute videos on YouTube. It should be fun!

I've sent an email to Margie in the Philippines (recommended by Laura) who will be typing up my recorded notes. I've got about 180 recorded memos so far, so that's quite a lot. I'm excited. I feel as if Christmas is coming and I've no idea what the present is going to look like, but I have this feeling that it'll be good. I declare that something huge is going to happen, that will set it all up. We'll see. I'm now on my way to my beautiful gym.

NOT DOING IT ON MY OWN

I have to say that I am grateful that I took the decision to hire someone to type those notes up for me. I could have done it myself. I can type.

But one thing that my previous job made me realise is the importance of delegating. Typing can be very time consuming. Besides, I do not enjoy it. So it's better spend my time on something I prefer doing, and that should improve the project's chances of succeeding. I know this might seem obvious to some of you, but for me this is a big deal. I am sure entrepreneurs can relate here. Most of us have started on our own. So you learn how to do everything. The biggest lesson for me so far as been to let go and delegate, to go much further. I think I have finally embraced this lesson. A successful project needs a team!

LOOKING FORWARD TO A MASTER CLEANSE

I've decided the next step for me is to do a Master Cleanse – I want to clean my body. In the last few days I've been eating bread and a couple of things that weren't raw, so I'm going to do just a little cleanse over, say, three or four days, to purify and detoxify my body. Yeah, just a short one, and then I'll spend a day coming off, drinking orange juice only that day, and then I'll be getting back to raw foods. I'll stop at Whole Foods on the way back from the gym to get what I need for it. (The only Whole Foods in London is just one tube stop away from where I live, and across from my gym!) Instead of buying just fruit and vegetables as usual, I'm going to buy maple syrup, lemons, and cayenne pepper. (If you want to learn more about it, just type 'Master Cleanse' into a search engine. There's a little book on it that costs $6 in the USA.) It's great! I did it about a year ago and it was amazing. It set me free of several addictions – tea, sugar, carbs. I no longer take sugar at all. Now I check the labels on things to make sure that I avoid processed food and eat healthily.

I just realised that it's the 1st of March. Happy March the 1st!

CLEANSING DEFERRED

I just got out of the gym and discovered, unfortunately, that Whole Foods was closed. Well, like most things in life, it depends how you take it. Since it opens at eight tomorrow morning I'll start the day with a little peppermint tea, then head to the gym for another session, then go and get what I need for the Master Cleanse. Off to a wonderful March!

MY COMPLEMENTARY FLATMATE HENRIK

My new flatmate, Henrik, is 40, and from Denmark. I was doing the feng shui on my room this afternoon, and he started to make a few changes to his too. He says it feels much better now. It's quite funny, really – the influence you have when you're on track, being your authentic self and following the Law of Attraction as diligently as I'm doing.

I am where I am because I've been practising the Law of Attraction for some time now, and, frankly if some people think it's a little bit 'out there' then it's just too bad. They could try it and see something wonderful develop, both magical and fun.

Anyway, I was telling Henrik yesterday that there's no such thing as coincidence in life, and that if we're living together right now, there's a reason for it. I don't know where it's going to lead, but it feels as if we are supposed to be in each other's company at this stage in our lives. Henrik has a great mind for technology and product development. He has some wonderful ideas and a very realistic and scientific perspective, so we kind of balance each other, in conversations at least. Yes, we've had some great conversations and, yes, we both have business minds, so it's all very interesting and I am looking forward to this new chapter of my life.

BEING 'IN THE ZONE'

When I consciously apply the Law of Attraction I feel 'in the zone'. It's a wonderful feeling. We have all experienced this. Sometimes it happens spontaneously, unexpectedly. It feels amazing – ideas flow and you are super-productive, creative and joyful. Everything seems to work out for the best. Well, this 'being in the zone' is how I have been feeling most of the time since I lost my job, deliberately applying the Law of Attraction and focusing on what feels good. Asking for more is essential. The Law of Attraction is always at work, whether you want it to be or not. It's like the law of gravity. Direct it and be conscious that it is working. Be aware of and manage your thoughts. You can go from declaring, asking and visualising to manifestation in the blink of eye. The clearer you are about what you want, and how it will feel, the faster you will be guided. It takes practice, but, I tell you, it creates miracles. Once in this flow, the way it's orchestrated seems divine. It's magical in that sense. I could never have dreamed of it happening like this. It is even better than I could have dreamed of!

YIN AND YANG

I believe all the pieces of a puzzle are coming together. And yes, we have to experience the hard times to recognise the good ones. There will always be good and bad. This is yin and yang.

Yin and yang, as described in Wikipedia (http://en.wikipedia.org/wiki/Yin_and_yang), are 'used to describe how seemingly disjunct or opposing forces are interconnected and interdependent in the natural world, giving rise to each other in turn'.

Yes, I had to experience the dissatisfaction and stress I had in my previous job – those unhappy moments – for me to know that I wanted something more fulfilling. Yes I had to be fired, and feel humiliated in front of my colleagues, for me to realise that I wanted something else, that I needed help, and that I wanted to help others full-time. I needed it to be able to appreciate every single step of the way now.

I felt so bad in my previous job, but I did not fully realise it when I was there – not to the extent I do now, anyway. Now I feel I am fully alive, and all my senses are awake.

LIVING WITH PEOPLE: MY GREAT FLATMATES!

8.15 a.m. I'm nearly at the gym. Henrik gave me this little book called *The Xenophobe's Guide to the Danes*. (Xenophobia, as they say in this book, is the irrational fear of foreigners.) There are similar little guides for other countries.

I'm an only child. I have no brothers or sisters, so I didn't really have that joy, that learning curve of sharing and being with others etc. My dream of living with others has always seemed far away. …Not any more, but for much of my life it felt like this unattainable thing. I thought that by living with housemates I would be able to learn how to share. Unlike with my career, though, I don't think I'll have to have a hard time to learn some lessons in this area! I've attracted these two wonderful flatmates, the second of whom is Giada from Italy, whom I've met only once, and who's in Milan at the moment.

Giada is 27 and works in the art industry. Funnily enough, both Henrik and Giada have lived in New York City, so all three of us had a US experience. We all like the USA. I learned so much there, and met some incredible people – incredible minds. I am eternally grateful to have spent time there, but I also appreciate being back in Europe. This place is so juicy and elegant at the same time! Especially London. I have always been lucky in England. At least this is how I feel, this is what I am thinking, and frankly, this is what is happening!

LIVING THE DREAM NOW?

…It doesn't have to be difficult to live with others. I've done it many times. Sometimes I can perhaps be too self-critical. Anyway, I'm realising that I'm living my dream right now. It doesn't have to be this remote thing in the distant future that one day I might just reach, when I have everything together. It can be right now!

Now I'm on Kensington High Street, passing Whole Foods where I'll go to get all the supplies for the Master Cleanse after my little workout. Speak to you soon!

DON'T LET YOUR WEAKNESSES OWN YOU

I'm back from the gym now, and all set for the Master Cleanse. I was thinking while I was on the Tube… Some people tell me my YouTube videos are so honest, authentic and real, but I think this book is the most authentic thing I've ever done. Yes, the videos are authentic, but they're just snapshots, short extracts from my life.

Certainly, if you really want to do this, if you really want to find your dream job, if you want to take your life on and transform it, you have to get real with yourself. You're going to have to face what's 'so' most of the time. Find out what is really happening. Our egos tend to hold us back from seeing what's really there, but I can assure you that you don't have to worry. It's not as if you're going to discover something awful about yourself. I know I can be bossy, controlling and very independent. I definitely have those characteristics, and it's important that I recognise them. Once you know your tendencies you can own them; they no longer own you. That's a clear and important distinction.

It's pointless copying other people's style, because it's likely you'll never do it as well as them; it's unique to them. For example, seeing my videos, some people say, 'Oh yeah, we want to do the same thing.' What I want to say is look for your own mode of expression, your own approach and perspective on things.

IDENTIFY AND CELEBRATE YOUR UNIQUE QUALITIES

What I am trying to say is that you should look at what makes you unique, and pursue that – go for it! Then you are likely to excel. You'll enjoy every single second. It won't feel like work. It'll be fun. Your creativity will be switched on. The benefits are just humungous! You won't be looking at the clock every few minutes. No. It's not fun when you cannot wait for your day's work to end. This was my experience in my last job. On two occasions during those six months I remember checking the time and wishing it was 5.30pm. Wow, that is so not like me! I am passionate. When I'm working I am usually oblivious of the time. When I was self-employed I often found myself working through the night. I was dedicated, and put in some good, solid graft. But, even then, I was not having fun. It wasn't all fun and play and delight, as it is supposed to be. (OK, yes, even in dream jobs there are always stressful moments. There are the hard times, but you go through them much more quickly and much more easily than anybody else when you love your job, and are on purpose.) So... what makes you unique?

PLAYFULNESS AND FUN: 'GO DUB YOURSELF!'

I often have to remind myself to be playful and childlike, to have fun. I can be too serious sometimes, you know. French people can be very serious – that's something for me to be conscious of. In fact, that's why I bought *The Artist's Way*. I am hoping to enhance my creativity, and do various little fun things.

Speaking of playfulness, my friend Hank Andries is a great example. He recently started – at 66 years of age – a chain of restaurants called 'Menna's Joint', where he serves 'dubs' (his unique take on the sandwiches most people know as 'subs'). The people working there (students) wear T-shirts with the slogan 'Go Dub Yourself'. I find it hilarious. He opened five of them over in Michigan in the past five years and now he is ready to conquer Europe. That's so exciting, and I'm so happy for him. He's a great role model and friend. To start a business like that at 66, and be that successful again, well, he's just so playful! He's like a kid. He's always giggling, and he doesn't take things seriously, and just moves on. I love him for that, and I feel honoured to know this man, a great example of playfulness and experimentation things and just, well, trying things on!

Hank did not need to start a new business for financial reasons. He had sold his first construction business in his thirties and was set for life. Maybe it's because he lost his dad when he was 14 that he learned how to deal with life differently, or maybe it's because he has a fascination for women, which led him to hide under his sister's bed when he was a kid and scare her half to death! But one thing is certain, no matter what Hank starts, you know he is going to have a fun time and be successful at it. He is very serious about business though, and a powerful entrepreneur. You'd better not mess with Hank, that is something I learned too! So try it yourself! Have fun! Why not? Is your life working that well right now? I mean, come on! I'm always ready to take on new things, and that's what makes life fun and juicy. Who knows what I'm going to take on this afternoon? Ha, ha!

F***!

I've just discovered that it takes two to three months to get a book formatted with BookSurge, the print-on-demand company that's part of Amazon – two to three months! That's much longer than

I'd thought. I'd wanted the book to be printed by mid-April, so, realistically, since we're at the beginning of March, that's not possible. Maybe there are some other options. Perhaps there are some other self-publishing print-on-demand companies that could do it more quickly.

But I have concerns about my income. So now I have my fears starting up again. I shall need to figure this out. According to BookSurge, from the moment the manuscript is finished to the moment it's printed, it takes two to three months. That's quite a long time. I shall just speak to them and see what possibilities we can create. Ideally no more than a month from completion to publication – that would be good. I'll check on the options.

You know that sucks! Two to three months! Ah, that's depressing. How am I going to do it? How am I going to make this happen? I want to get published, and to make sure the process is rolling. I feel lost. I feel depressed. All of a sudden, it's so negative, so I'm going to see if the natural world can make me feel a bit better. I'm walking to the little private park we share with some neighbours.

A NATURE-AND-BOOK BREAK, AND BATTLING WORRIES

I'm now in the park. I brought a couple of my new books, *The Artist's Way*, and the *Petit Cahier d'Exercices d'Estime de Soi*, with its little exercises on self-esteem. Boy, things don't feel good right now, and I need to switch that energy.

Without the reading, I must admit I would feel that I was wasting time. I feel the pressure of a lot of stuff that I need to get done, and I'm getting worried as far as finances are concerned – where is the money going to come from? I need at least another month to finish the manuscript of this book, so we're looking at three to four months to get it published. I cannot hold out three to four months with the money I have in my account at the moment.

Anyway, I'm going to breathe deeply – in and out – enjoy nature, calm down and do some reading.

Now I'm thinking that maybe I should have a publisher to manage all this. I don't know how to handle this situation. There seem to be so many things think of. I should at least reconsider the possibility of finding a publisher. I know that everything is happening for the best, so if I'm getting this warning, there is a reason. I should probably be examining some aspect of this in a bit more depth. At least I'm moving forward with the manuscript; that side of the things should be finished by the end of March. I should consider all my options, and do one thing at a time.

OK, two to three months. I wanted the book to be published by the 24th of April. That's not going to happen. So am I still going to go ahead with all the events? Should I still have this big CCOR thing in London? The list of things to do is long, and I don't want to pick any kind of job just to get some money in, so I'm asking for higher guidance. Please, greater Self, source, energy... help me find my way here. I receive all the abundance now.

But part of me just wants to get to work, and go and get the facts and figures (How much will it cost to get the book out earlier? Could another printer do it? If so, when...?) and do, do, do, but this is not how the Law of Attraction works, so that's why I'm stopping everything, and doing these exercises to shift my energy, and to find my way back to feeling inspired again, to being clear on what I'm going to take on next. Yes, I'm a long way from that clarity, so I might as well just stop everything, and simply sit here in my little park, reading inspirational books and doing the exercises they suggest.

BEYOND THE WALL

It's maddening that I cannot get the idea out of my head, that after all that's happened, I appear to have hit this wall. There must be a reason for this. Everything that's happened up to this point was needed for me to learn something. I should be responsible for declaring what I want, and put everything in place as if I were 100% certain, but there's still part of me that doubts. How would things be if I threw myself 100% into this? ...Took everything to a whole new level? Part of me is scared about taking on such a challenge, because I have a tendency to hedge my bets, to do things provisionally, but I don't think this is the appropriate attitude now. I want to pump it up, and really play this Law of Attraction to the maximum. I might need to do that. It's 3.11 – yes, that 11 again! I must be on track! ☺

BUILDING SELF-ESTEEM AND READING

All right, it's now 3.22, so that means I spent 20 minutes in the park, and I definitely feel more relaxed. The little book on self-esteem was *genial*!

DON'T TAKE 'NO' FOR AN ANSWER: GOOD NEWS

It is important not to get stopped, isn't it? Well, I decided not to just accept what I read on the BookSurge website (that it would take two to three months, which for me is just too big a delay). I called them in the US. I want to make it happen, I want to have the printed book in my hands by April 24th. I spoke with a BookSurge representative and through talking to her I was able to reduce the time by two or three weeks. This means 'expediting the system' – a lot more coordination, planning and focus, and more money – but it is possible. The idea now is to attract the finances.

FIGHTING DOUBTS AGAIN

I declare that I will enrol someone, or receive help, or get some money somehow to help me finance this, and make it happen. I strongly believe in it, but I'm also conscious, putting the figures together, that this is a gamble. I think I'm ready to do it because I feel strongly about it, but I just want to make sure I don't crash… I strongly believe in what I'm doing, but also must be realistic… but I also know that abundance is our birthright, and money is just energy, and if I need the money, the money will come if I allow it to. Yes, I have to get out of the way, and stop thinking in a limiting way: that this is not possible based on what I see in my bank account! So I am making it happen, you know! I know it will happen, and that's what I need to focus on right now in order to be successful. Also, I have always asked financial help around me. This time I want to do be resourceful. I know I can attract the money I need without asking for anyone's help around. The money can come from many different sources that I am not even aware off. Money is energy, and it is not my duty to worry about it. I have to say that this feel really to me like a quantum leap I am making. I have faith it will all work out.

JUST ALLOW IT!

I have this little yellow bottle on my desk, and the logo is this little cartoonish guy with his arms in the air and he's just letting himself slide down this little river, and below the river are the words 'Just allow it' (http://justallowit.com/order-allow/), like the 'Just do it' Nike tagline. The bottle supposedly contains this substance called 'ALLOW!', and this is the brainchild of my friend, Fred Morton, whom I met in the Chicago Law-of-Attraction meet-up group www.meetup.com. Of course, there isn't really anything inside the bottle, and yet there's everything! I just love that idea. The label says:

This product is not intended to replace anything you are taking or doing. Just replace with what you're thinking. Direction for

use: Allowing is the quickest way to return to your wellness,
change your manifestations and achieve your desires.
There is only one stream and that is a stream of wellness.
Let go of the resistant thoughts that are keeping you from
becoming the person you truly desire to be, by reaching
your thoughts that brings you emotional relief now, and the
stream of wellness will carry you towards your desires.

Great! I just love it, and I had quite a few bottles of ALLOW! around my home in Chicago. I used to have one in my bathroom, so every time I looked in the mirror and saw spots coming out, or little wrinkles developing, every time I caught myself thinking negatively about myself, I would just think, 'I should apply a little bit of ALLOW!' and this would smooth my day. It gave me permission to shift my way of thinking.

So I think right now it's time for me to take a big dose of ALLOW! and regain my faith. I know this is a struggle for many of us. Fear creeps in all too easily after the 'Ah-I-lost-my-job!' moment, when you need to get going, when you need to find money, when you need to do something… and so just to allow things to happen is a big shift in thinking. I'm not saying just sit at home and do nothing while changing your thinking, but new things can happen if you apply a bit of ALLOW! You will see things shifting and new ideas coming in.

So, I'm going to allow the abundance of Life to come to me and help me in putting this project – this amazing project – together so that I can live my dream and empower millions of people, and I ask for support. Here we go. I apply a big dose of ALLOW! Ha, ha!

PRAYING TO GOD

I don't often use the word 'God' but I really want to pray right now and say:

Dear God, please make this happen. Help me and support me in every single way. Allow me to be creative and resourceful, and to find the money and the energy to put this project in place on time, and to deliver it to the millions of people in the world who need this support right now. Please allow me to make this book a great book. Something that will help people see the possibilities for new beginnings in their lives – fresh starts. Please let them see through these lines that there is something waiting for them, something that's just made for them, and please give those people the courage to see and follow their dreams and their passions. Please allow them to find their missions and be true to themselves. Please give them the confidence. Please give them the courage. Please help them to see the light.

THE AVOCADO IMAGE

A while ago I had this idea of the image of an avocado on the book cover. I have to think why this got stuck in my mind.

Today is the 3rd of March. Last time I left off with my little avocado idea. Of course I love eating avocados. I think it's a 'juicy' thing, in my sense of the word. I think avocado flesh is so rich, and then the middle part – that hard part – could represent the globe, but I haven't figured out why an avocado? Perhaps its richness symbolises the richness of life. I'm not sure why the planet should be inside it.

RECOGNISING SABOTAGING THOUGHTS

When I woke up this morning, I found myself thinking about the way thoughts can sabotage you. You know, for example, I might declare something like, 'I declare that I want money coming in, and help and finances to make this project come true,' but in the back of my mind, I am saying, 'Yeah, right. It won't happen.' And sometimes there's also this conversation along the lines of 'But is this really what I want?' Of course these thoughts then prevent things from manifesting, so I have come to the conclusion that either I go for it 100%, and say, 'Yeah, this is really what I want. This is really it.' or I decide that it's just not it for me.

MINOR PROGRESS

I'm also working on the title of the book, and getting some input on this from my friends Daniel and Hank. I also let them have a sneak peek at the first few pages so that they could give me some feedback.

I'm going to go to the gym. This morning I had a couple of phone calls, but it wasn't particularly productive – just some things I needed to do. That makes me think: what does it mean 'to be productive'? You know what? I *am* moving forward and things *are* happening! So I am being productive after all!

DEFINING MY DREAM

I'm back to defining my dream. What is my dream? I have been saying for many years that my dream is to help millions of people live with passion and on purpose. I want to empower millions of people daily – OK, but why? Well, one thing is that I want people to be happy, to be joyful in their lives, and I think if everybody does what they're meant to do then there is more peace on this planet. People wouldn't be fighting for things (or at least there would be a lot less fighting) because everybody would be doing what they wanted. Do I need a reason beyond that? This is what I want to do, but then how am I actually going to empower millions of people? Yes, my videos are viewed online by thousands of people every day (my videos on http://youtube.com/liloumace have received to date over 1.8 million views, without being featured by YouTube once!

The 'Co-Creating Our Reality' community is definitely another way in which I am empowering people, but what does it take to go from thousands to millions daily?

BREAKTHROUGH: THE MISSING PIECE OF THE DECLARATION!

This is pretty bold, what I'm about to declare, but this is it – I might as well apply the Law of Attraction fully – so, on this third day of March 2009, I declare that I will empower millions of people daily very soon – very, very soon. I'm opening myself to receive ideas on how this can happen. I used to think, many years ago, before doing seminars, that it was a question either of making a difference or making money, but that you couldn't do both. Now, however, I'm clear that those things are totally compatible: you can do both at the same time! So my idea is to empower millions (of people) and make millions (of dollars, pounds, euros…), and you know, I don't have to apologise for wanting to make money, because money lets you help others, and be there for them, and there are so many ways to do that… I was brought up Catholic, and, sometimes, I think, we Catholics have this difficulty… this strange perception of money, but, no, my declaration has been made: I will empower millions *and* make millions. I think the last bit was the part that was missing and inauthentic in what I was saying before. I still want to empower millions, and neither part of the declaration detracts in the slightest from the other. Yeah, it feels good! It feels liberating to say that, to tell you the truth – definitely more authentic. So how is that going to happen? I have no idea yet, and I'm open to guidance, and to seeing how all this is going to unfold.

MORE ON THE AVOCADO IDEA

All right, so here's the latest... I did a little research on avocados, because, for some reason, I still have this image of an avocado in my head, and, as you know, I just love them. I did a Google search on avocado, and I found this image of a woman with her bare back towards the viewer, and in her hand she's holding half an avocado, cut lengthwise with the stone showing. I like that image very much! I think it's beautiful and provocative at the same time, and would be completely appropriate because the book is pretty much an open journey. Steven Martine www.StevenMartine.com, a good friend of mine and an excellent photographer, would be great for this! He is in Florida right now, but I know he'd do a great job.

FEELING LIBERATED

Since I restated my dream – my dream job – I feel really liberated. It feels as if the missing piece was simply the statement that I will empower millions and make millions. I wasn't allowing myself to say it, because it felt wrong earlier. Now I actually feel very good about it, and I can now move wholeheartedly towards bringing it about. Possibly I'll do a video about this, because I think once we are honest with ourselves about what we really want, then things can really happen, and happen fast. So I'm definitely open to seeing how I can empower millions *and* make millions, and this is the dream I'm taking on. This is the Law of Attraction here at work, so let's see how this unfolds.

SEEKING DESIGNERS AND ARRANGING A PHOTOGRAPHER

Now I'm looking to attract the cover designer and the interior book designer as well, and I have a couple of contacts, so I'm looking forward to attracting that person very soon!

Regarding Steven Martine, I'm going to check the flights now to see if I can fly him into London. Otherwise I was thinking of going to Florida myself, but I think it would be better for him to come to London. That way we could do some London publicity shots. My last photo shoot was on the Fort Lauderdale beach in Florida, off the A1A. I could definitely use some pictures of London – promotional pictures and one for the cover of the book, of course, and some for the website... So I'm going to look into the flights. It would be super-exciting to have him come over and show him around London, and, at the same time, do the photo shoot.

ON TRACK AGAIN

I'm just fascinated how things are coming together. Right now I'm considering the logistics of a CCOR meeting in London: getting everybody together and offering them the book. When I look at the package, it's as if all the elements, and all the people that I need to put it together, are just coming to me. For example, the hotel: I'm thinking, OK, I need a hotel, maybe a budget hotel or a central hotel, which then makes me think of Hyde Park, which would be a great area. Then I think, well, back in May when I came to London for the first time, for a weekend visit, I met Jane, and she has a home – a beautiful home, a peaceful mansion – that would be perfect for this. I'm going to check the number of rooms it has, but this is a very strong possibility. It's as if the answer has come easily and magically. The full team is coming together for everything that I need, whether it's the interior of the book, whether it's for this CCOR project. It feels like I'm on track again now.

PUSHING THE LIMITS

I just received this email from a friend:

> *My friend,*
> *I appreciate your work. Every time I'm in contact with Lewis,*
> *I think of you. A few days ago I got an email (below) from my*
> *friend Lewis containing a video link to CNN. I thought it might*
> *be interesting for you. (Lewis is a special person and I think*
> *you are too.)*
> *Best wishes*

I clicked on this CNN video called 'pushing the limits' - *CNN's Robyn Curnow reports on Lewis Pugh's drive to push his body and mind to swim in the world's coldest waters* (http://edition.cnn.com/video/#/video/international/2009/02/27/vital.signs.pushing.limit.bk.a.cnn). The video is about pushing the limits, and the man in question is Lewis Pugh. Lewis contacted me shortly after I arrived in London. He told me that he was using visualisation in his long distance swims and, in particular, that it helped him become the first person to undertake a long distance swim at the North Pole; he really swims in those extreme conditions! His nickname is 'the polar bear'. Look him up (http://www.lewispugh.com/). He's doing extraordinary work and enjoys pushing his boundaries to raise awareness about the fragility of our environment and to encourage everyone to take action. It turned out that Lewis had found my videos on YouTube and knew I was in London, so I had the opportunity of meeting him. What a treat!

In this video he emphasises the importance of visualisation. Before he enters those freezing waters (which can kill people very easily), he visualises everything vividly. He tastes the salty waters in his mouth. He feels the ice burning his skin. He lives those moments when he

his

will swim the North Pole, hundreds and hundreds of time in ~~my~~ mind. That's how he prepares for a swim.

He shared with me his stories of training with the Kayak Olympic teams to prepare for his next challenge – all of which were very insightful. I drank in every word. I could not believe that such a handsome, gentle and passionate man would be interested in meeting me. And he sure was – his intention was clear – he was there to deliver a message. He thinks I have a gift for guided visualisations. With committed practice, he says, I could excel at it. He encouraged me to give it 110%. Needless to say I was so honoured to receive such a compliment from someone who has worked closely with Al Gore, Tony Blair and Gordon Brown, to name a few of the people he knows personally.

Lewis is a fantastic example of how athletes – or should I say champions (people who push their limits in general) – use the power of visualisation.

So, why wouldn't we want to use it in our daily lives, to help us reach our goals and dreams much more quickly?

STEVEN MARTINE

I said I was considering flying Steven over from Florida to shoot the cover pics for the book and take some general promotional photos. I've checked the web now and identified some potential flights next weekend. It's not something I had originally planned to spend money on, but I think that good pictures make a tremendous difference.

I have to cancel this thought, because I do want somebody amazing to design this, but I have a feeling the person I originally had in mind might be too expensive, or not able to deliver it on time, and

I must make sure that everything is aligned. I have to cancel that thought again! I will attract a talented designer who will be within my budget.

YES, IT'S REALLY OK TO MAKE MONEY!

Yesterday, when I was putting together the CCOR package for the weekend getaway in London, and trying to get people to come to it, and planning the launch event itself, I realised how much work it all was. I was thinking, then, is it OK for me to make a profit from this? I must take on board the fact that my time is valuable, and if I set everything up then I have to put a price on the time involved to do it. So this is one of the lessons I need to learn, on the way to realising my dream of making a difference *and* making money. I remind myself of the feeling of liberation I had when I declared that I wanted to empower millions and make millions. But right now I am thinking from a perspective of lack.

Another breakthrough is needed here I think! I am going to repeat to myself the following affirmation: 'I am worthy and deserving…' or maybe even write it on my bathroom mirror as Kevin Ross, author of *Live the Designer Life*, recommended to me in November 2003 during his workshop in Miami. Actually, it is in this workshop that I created my first mission statement, which was:

My mission is to enrol, create and produce positive forms of media that leave people inspired, joyful and fulfilled.

LIVING THE DREAM JOB

I am so much more confident than I was three weeks ago, when I was in that draining job. Two different Lilous! Only three weeks later it's wonderful to see how I'm putting all this together, knowing that I have the skills to make it a huge success. I feel that I'm so on track.

STAYING IN LONDON WAS THE RIGHT DECISION

I'm really thankful for having this place here, and that I moved here instead of going to France, or pursuing some other ideas I had. I feel really creative and just so good here! The apartment is beautiful, and this and the gym are truly anchoring me and helping me live from perspective of abundance. So I'm very thankful that I took that path I did, because otherwise my mind and world would have shrunk, and I'd be in scarcity mode. Right now, by contrast, I really feel – and constantly remind myself – that it's OK, that things are working out as they are meant to, that extraordinary things are happening, and that I'm open to guidance at every single stage.

A SERIES OF BOOKS?

I'm loving the process of putting this book together so much that I'm already clear that I want to do another one very soon; it's so helpful for me right now in my life, a great support. I could produce a whole series of books of this nature – a Juicy Living Series or something. Now, that's juicy! I can see myself starting the next one immediately after I've finished this one.

PUBLICITY AND MARKETING IDEAS

I've compiled a list of all the people I want to give the book to, who will be referenced in it as well. I'm going to send it to Oprah Winfrey, John Gray, Deepak Chopra, Sonia Choquette, Sandy Grason, Laura Duksta, and Lewis Pugh. It makes sense to spread the word to people who have a big reach, as they do, and I also hope to get their feedback, and quotes and/or reviews. All going well, with their help I'll build a lot of support. I'm creating the possibility of a lot of help from many people.

MORE PROGRESS ON THE BOOK

Yesterday – Tuesday – I called Gerry Hillman, one of my editor's friends. Eric suggested that Gerry might be able to design the interior of the book, so I called him right away. He seems to be the right person, and he should be able to do the work in the time required, so I'm very relieved to have found him.

Regarding the cover, I haven't yet attracted exactly who's going to do that, but I'm going to draft out my ideas, and have a look at various books and titles and fonts. I've already found the format that I want – that of Chris Dines' *Power, Love and Abundance*.

A SEVEN-DAY CLEANSE

Did I say I love avocado? Well, I'm on Master Cleanse, Day 3, so no avocado right now. I feel that I'm ridding my body of all the toxins in it by drinking this maple syrup, cayenne pepper and lemon juice, and it feels wonderful. I'm extending the cleanse to seven days, even though I've organised a singles' party on Friday. By then I'll be coming out of it on nothing but orange juice, but I'll still have a lot of fun. No alcohol, of course, but I really feel that I should continue the cleanse, because it feels great.

HOW AND WHY I CAME TO LONDON

We have to tap into a greater power than ourselves – to use the Law of Attraction – because otherwise life would be a struggle. I landed my London job in the first place purely by applying the Law of Attraction.

The story goes back to when I studied at Oxford Brookes University in '98 and '99, as part of my European Business Studies programme (most of which was in France). Then, in May 2008, after almost ten years away from England, I decided to pay a weekend visit to see the country again, as well as my childhood friend, Geraldine, whom I grew up with in Nantes, and who had just given birth to baby girl named Lola.

After visiting her in Brighton, and my college sweetheart, Kai, in London, I decided that it was time for me to come back. Although after my London weekend I spent some time in France visiting my mom, I immediately started to look for a job in England, and applied for a handful of positions. Then, shortly after I got back to the USA, I remember declaring very powerfully that I wanted a well-paid job in London, where everything would work out for me, and this is exactly what I got. A week later I received an email from Genevieve, whom I really have to acknowledge. I must thank her for getting me the job, and I'm going to contact her because I feel as if that chapter – of my London job – isn't completely resolved. I want to thank her for hiring me, and explain what's transpired. This way I will feel a sense of closure. I think there's an important point here – if you're going through something similar, you want to make sure that you're 'complete' with everybody, that everything has been said and acknowledged. Do it when you can come from a place of gratitude, for what you have learned and for where you are now going. I think there's a lot to be said for resolving your past in this way.

Anyway, getting back to this job... I got this email shortly after I had made my declaration, and then after several telephone interviews with my future boss to be, Peter (the CEO of the company), I landed the position. I knew this was the job I wanted to attract, and so did Peter. We did not have to meet in person. A month later, I had packed my bags, sold all my belongings and car, found people to take over my office and apartment lease, as well as my business accounts – all using the Law of Attraction of course! I then spent six months with the company, during which time I learned so many of the lessons I needed to learn in order to make this next chapter in my life a really successful one, so I'm very grateful for that experience.

I feel so in the flow, I cannot even sleep. I'm so excited. I wake up so early in the morning, ideas flowing through my mind. It's to promote and sustain this creativity that I'm now reading *The Artist's Way*, and I start on Week 1 of the book's programme this week. I'm just feeling great, living my dreams and following my passion.

MANAGING THE HIGHS AND THE LOWS

It is important, however, to balance the high energy also, because I have a tendency, for example, to get very excited about things and my energy levels shoot up and then... This is the balance of Life. I learned this particularly from Laura, who learned it from Dr John Demartini. So it's important to learn to balance the good news and the bad, because things happen in our day-to-day lives that will bring us back down from great highs. In other words, it's important to cultivate stable energy, and I am learning how to be more in control of this. One way of doing it, which I have found to be quite effective, is to have several projects on the go. For example, right now, yes, I'm still chasing a TV career, but I'm also working on the book and the CD, so these things are balancing each other. In this way, good news on one front may counteract bad news on another. It's important not to put all your eggs in one basket, as they say, and to have several balancing options to take that pressure off (making sure, therefore, that the pressures from these various projects will not be additive), and to help you find the right energy to just continue cruising horizontally. Does this make sense?

I feel that the more I practise, the fewer lows I experience; that my energy levels are more stable and things feel better. With practice I am able to shift my energy more quickly. All the practices I am sharing in this book help me maintain this steady energy. It works! I just love it! It is such juicy stuff, guys!

THERE ARE NO COINCIDENCES

I hope this book is clearly demonstrating how to use the Law of Attraction. It doesn't require a lot of work. Yes, there are many aspects to it, but once you're in it, it just flows, and you're inspired to the next action, and you feel good about it. It's not a struggle. It's not a to-do list. It's about being fully part of the unfolding of things. Yes, it does involve some work. You can't just sit there and daydream, but as you can see, the whole process is a delight, and things fall into place at the right time – everything comes. I know that if you have attracted this book into your life and you are now reading it, it's no coincidence. This is going to put you on the path, and you now have a choice of moving forward and learning from this experience as you apply it in your own life... or not.

A FREE GUIDED VISUALISATION FOR MANIFESTING A JUICY LIVING!

I'm going to add a list of useful books to mywebsite (www.LilouMace. com). I came across many of them through practising the Law of Attraction. I recommend you read them, particularly if you're a beginner and ready to take this on. Also, as part of the meditation I'm about to record, I'll do a guided visualisation for those of you who want to attract a juicy living – something you can visualise and listen to every day. You will be able to download it free from the home page of my website, LilouMace.com. I'll place a button there and you can download it and listen to it as an mp3 – put it on your iPod or your computer, have it handy. Starting your mornings with it would be very powerful. This will be one of one of the tracks on my visualisation CD, but I'm offering it to everyone who has purchased the book because I'm committed to everyone manifesting the job of their dreams! When you click on the button you'll need to enter a code, and the code will be... AVOCADO, of course!

THE IMPORTANCE OF LETTING GO AND BEING OPEN

You know this whole process has been a constant reminder to me of the importance of letting go. At every single little baby step my mind has been running towards finding a conclusion to this or that... and so I constantly have to bring myself back to the present moment. It's OK not to have the answers. Just by asking for them, you can have them really fast. This approach is helpful in stopping you in coming to conclusions like 'This is not possible' or 'I'm not finding this' or 'I'm never going to get this' or 'I'll never find the job of my dreams' or 'reality has proven to me this this is not possible', ' no one has done this before'.

No, as soon as you catch that negative thought then cancel it and say 'Cancel, cancel' and then recreate it: 'I'm open to finding an answer for this. I'm open to seeing how I can finance this project. I'm open to seeing how I can meet the right people. I'm open to....' Just say: 'I'm open to seeing this situation from a new perspective.'

RELAXING MUSIC

I'm now listening to Naiki, *Canyon Trilogy*. It's very relaxing music. This CD was offered to me by Nina and Marcel. They are good friends of the family and guides in the Zion National Park in Utah. I play it when I want to focus on things and really get cooking as they say. That's an expression from my friend Hank, by the way: 'Yes, we're cooking, Lilou.' I once read that soothing music slows your heart and helps you relax, and when you're more relaxed you retain information better and you're more able to focus, so I used to put this music on in the background when I was studying. Now I use it when I'm working on my various projects.

FINDING SUPPORT FROM THE CCOR COMMUNITY

I truly believe in the power of community and that if I was able to attract so much juiciness in my life it is because of each and every member of the '100-Day Reality Challenge' community. I think it's important to get ongoing support, and that's one of the things that is really working well right now with creating this book: the project is building support through my application of the Law of Attraction. I encourage you to join 'Co-Creating Our Reality' community. It's booming! Registration is free, and so if you want to apply the Law of Attraction and get the free support you need, go to CoCreatingOurReality.com. Thousands of people in 125 countries are doing this over sessions (seasons) of 100 days. All you need to do is create your profile and then when you start a new 100-day session that becomes your Season 1. I'm currently on Season 11, and so that means I've completed the '100-Day Reality Challenge' ten times. Every time you do it you create goals and intentions. You could certainly have the intention to find your dream job in 100 days! You have the opportunity of blogging and video-blogging during every 100-day season, which leads directly to people within the community giving you support. I also find it extremely powerful to declare out loud to the community your goals, intentions and declarations. There are also many resources: a lot of information, book recommendations, and discussions, such as how to get started. You name it, you'll find it there.

ANOTHER POSSIBLE SELF-PUBLISHING PRINT-ON-DEMAND COMPANY

I just had a conversation with Sarah, leading consultant with BookSurge. I asked her for more details related to the flexibility I will have to access my own account on Amazon, namely adding my own video trailer of the book. I was disappointed to hear there was none. Then I asked her about the possibility to upload the audio version of the book. Her answer confirmed to me that BookSurge was not an option for me. She told me to check the Amazon Affiliate programme, which led me to CreateSpace (www.CreateSpace. com). And there was THE solution I had been looking for: no set-up cost and only two weeks to get online and have copies of my book. Therefore it'll be ready in good time for the London Book Fair. ☺ This is such a relief!

FEELINGS OF SUCCESS

I really feel that this is going to be a great success. I feel so much in the flow – that this project is aligned with everything that I've wanted, that I'm not allowing my fears to get in the way, and that I am moving forward with confidence. This feels so great that the outcome can only be wonderful. I feel I'm now attracting everything that I need with no difficulty: all the people and all the resources. That doesn't mean no work – I can tell you I'm working very late at night to make this happen – but it's such a delight and so much fun to focus on what's possible instead of always creating additional obstacles, so I'm very grateful for this experience.

STARTING THE DAY WITH A SONG

I woke up this morning singing, 'Le soleil vient de se lever, encore une belle journée,, l'ami du petit déjeuner, l'ami Ricoré.' French people would know what I'm talking about here, but years and years ago this was a TV ad in France for a brand of coffee. Sometimes it's a song that puts you in a good mood. Translated into English the words would be: 'The sun has just risen, another beautiful day, my breakfast friend, my friend Ricoré.' Now there are several things that are not physically relevant to me here. There is practically no sun in England. I'm not having any breakfast because I'm doing the Master Cleanse (Day 4 now), and I don't drink coffee. *Yes, I'm French, but I only drink tea.* Nevertheless, when it comes to emotion, that song hits the spot every time I sing it. What could put you into such a good mood at the start of your day?

LUNCHING WITH THE CO-CEO OF WAYN

I just had lunch (well, peppermint tea for me), as planned, with Jerome Touze in a friendly Italian restaurant. He's the Co-CEO of WAYN (www.wayn.com), which has grown from 45,000 users in March 2005 to over 13 million today. What a fantastic story he's got there! Anyway, the guy's 29 years old and he started WAYN on the side with two friends while he was working in London as a consultant for a big consulting firm, and he is now one of the most respected people in the industry.

Jerome believes that what goes around, comes around, and has always lived his life according to those principles. He's a very open, charming French guy – and single, ladies!

ANOTHER PHOTOGRAPHER?

Now I'm on my way back home, and continuing to unleash the potential of the Law of Attraction – living it. I'm putting the CCOR event together, and attracting the designer of the cover, the interior of the book, and the photographer. I contacted my friend, the photographer Steven Martine, and he can't come, but I received an email from another photographer, based in England, and I spoke with her, and it turns out that her student might be the perfect person for this, and so I'm considering getting him on board. He's here in London, so that would work nicely, so I'm finalising that.

I'm interviewing Brian Johnson of *PhilosophersNotes* for a five-minute YouTube video, and then, in the afternoon, I'm going to a seminar about the earth, which should be pretty inspiring. I look forward to it.

DON'T STOP ASKING!

You know, yesterday I noticed a kind of 'plateau-ing out' of my activity levels. I was doing things – I've been really working, and doing, doing, doing – but I noticed a kind of a dip in my energy levels, even though I was feeling good about doing what I was doing. What occurred to me this morning is that I had stopped asking. I think this is an important point, because, to be sustained, energy constantly needs to be in motion, and if you stop asking, then you stop getting, and so it's about constantly asking for more, whether for guidance or something else. If I don't continue now to ask for other elements – to pull myself constantly into the flow by asking and dreaming – then I'm pulling myself out of the flow and, therefore, things begin to feel a little flat.

So I'm opening myself up again to keep on asking and being in that mode of enquiry. I'm striving to dream even more, and, in particular, I'm opening myself up to finding, to attracting the title of my book. I would like to attract the title to me such that it's completely clear to me what it should be. I want a title that will speak to millions of people, that will fit with the cover of the book and the content, and that will entice many people to buy it because they will understand from it that the book has the content that they need right now.

NEW PHOTOGRAPHER, NEW IDEAS

I've been speaking withthe photography student, Jack Latimer (www.laterus.co.uk). As a photographer I'm sure he can guide me to some extent, but I'm going to do some thinking here, and some allowing. I also want to attract the designer of the cover, because up until now I've been resisting it a bit, so it's not really happening. Maybe this will flow a little bit better when I have the pictures, when I see that I have the cover picture right there in front of me, so it's probably OK not to worry right now. I'm just taking things one step at a time, and allowing it to happen in the natural flow of events.

ANTICIPATING THE BRIAN JOHNSON INTERVIEW

I'm getting ready to interview Brian Johnson at 9 o'clock – in 40 minutes. He is the founder of www.PhilosophersNotes.com with his 52 downloads of some awesome books that I really recommend you download. I'm going to ask Brian about how he got started and how he manages to be so productive, because he's achieved so much, and I also want to know what his favourite book is, and what is next for him. It will be a five-minute interview and I'll post it on my YouTube channel. I am looking forward to what will be great interview. In five minutes he will provide a lot of information that will be useful to many people. I have a feeling there will be some great online interaction.

IT'S NOT WRONG TO WANT MORE

My mom used to tell that I'd never be satisfied, that I was constantly dreaming, and now that I think about, if this is how I was raised, it's not surprising that part of me always felt it was wrong to be asking for more. Now, however, through this process, I'm realising how important it is to keep asking and dreaming, that asking is actually the essence of life. This is what we're here for. I don't think we should feel guilty about wanting more. What we should do, by contrast, is allow ourselves to welcome more into our life as we ask for it!

BRIAN JOHNSON: AN INSPIRING INTERVIEW

I just interviewed Brian Johnson. This interview can be found at http://www.youtube.com/watch?v=6ZyUxy-FieA.

I feel so fortunate to have met in two days two very powerful, successful leaders, who not only have prosperous businesses but are also making a huge positive difference to the world.

Brian was a part of Zaadz.com that got sold to Gaia.com, which is a huge inspirational community out there. He sold that business in 2007, then decided to start recording all those books, and condense the big ideas from them. They're the most amazing self-development books you can find. I've read most of them, but don't you think it's a great idea to condense each of them into 18-minute single mp3s? So, for example, he has on there *The Seven Spiritual Laws of Success* by Deepak Chopra, *The Seven Habits of Highly Effective People* by Stephen Covey, *The Power of Intention* by Wayne Dyer, *The New Earth* by Eckhart Tolle, *Ask and It is Given* by Esther and Jerry Hicks, *The Secret of the Millionaire's Mind* by T. Harv Eker. All those amazing books! I feel so fortunate to have had the opportunity of having met him like that, and to have the technology that allows it, because he's in Bali and I interviewed him from London.

BRIAN RECOMMENDS DAILY MEDITATION

He only recently decided to move to Bali, by the way. He lived in Los Angeles but moved to Bali to focus on his business and do these recordings, and enjoy his time. Interestingly, though, he said that it took him seven years before he really found his passion. He apparently practises meditation every day. For him it's for an hour, but he recommends that each of us find the practice that suits us, and that we could continue to do on a regular basis. There's a certain discipline to all this, of course. There are all those tools and techniques, and I think eventually it just comes. Again, though, if you don't know what practice really works for you, and don't recognise when it feels right, then just ask for guidance, and be willing and open to finding what it could be, and at least commit to one form of it. For example, I have those little visualisations. I do them for ten minutes a day, or I do reiki, or I do the videos as part of the '100-Day Reality Challenge'. Those are some of the things that keep me on track in the long term.

Anyway, Brian, well done! I think you're a fantastic example of what's possible when we open ourselves up to the possibility of having unlimited power and letting it all flow in, and enjoying our authentic selves.

RESISTING THE TEMPTATION TO LEAVE MY NATURAL PATH

I just received an email from Chenelle (http://www.cocreatingourreality. com/profile/Chenelle). She's one of the UK members of 'Co-Creating Our Reality', and also the person who has offered to keep the updates going on our CCOR Twitter account (www.twitter.com/ccor). She writes: 'I'm not sure if you're still in the web design business but I have this person looking for a web site for £3,000.'

You know what? It is so tempting for me right now to reply, 'Yes, I'm going to do it,' but I just said no, even though I need that kind of money. I do know, though, this would derail me. I want to really up the ante now in manifesting abundance and ideas, and setting everything up to win at my own game, following my own passion and making this happen, so I turned it down. Despite that, I must admit that it feels like it's a moment-to-moment thing; I'm still drawn, to some extent, to tempting job offers (guaranteed financial security!) and away from my natural path, which is what I'm following right now. (I censored myself there: I stopped myself saying that the natural thing would be to go for the ready money!) It's happening for me, but there's this automatic or conditioned response built into us by society to go for the secure (spirit-crushing?) job that I must resist. No, I'm fully committed right now to living this greatness, to living on purpose, and to allowing myself to win this game and make a wonderful living from doing what I love.

THE 'WHAT ON EARTH ARE WE DOING?' EVENT

I'm on my way to the 'What On Earth Are We Doing?' event. They're doing a 'world tour' (Hong Kong, Sydney and London) and I'm here for the entire afternoon, all the way through until 9.30 p.m.

We're just having a little break right now from the 'Be the Change' symposium here in Earl's Court in London, and I am so thankful to be here and be part of this discussion. I have shivers running through my body, and it's so much the perfect time. This symposium is mainly about environmental change, and the spiritual and social justice changes that need to happen to this world for our lives to be sustainable. An absolutely wonderful conversation just took place, with thousands of attendees.

We talked about dreams, for example. There are so many things that we want – we want more of this and more of that – and a lot of those things are material, when really there's something else that needs fulfilling inside us. They spoke about dreams, but in the sense of being an awake dreamer. This is how I have been feeling since I started on this adventure, and started writing this book. It's finally waking me up to the bad things that are happening out there, and, simultaneously to the possibilities for making things better in the world, and to the positive transformations that are occurring.

Each and every one of us has a role to play. I want to ask you, 'What is your role on this planet? Where do you want to be? What do you want to teach your great grandchildren? What do you want to tell them when they ask, "What difference did you make?"'

This is the kind of conversation happening in that room, and it's really wonderful being part of this and looking at all of it and feeling that we are one. I'm definitely clear about that: we are one.

ALLOWING LIFE TO FLOW THROUGH US

Lynne Twist, Roger Hamilton, and Marcia Martin were three absolutely phenomenal speakers!

Marcia explained the developmental stages in our lives (some of us are victims, and then we move to realising that we're 100% responsible for where we're at, and then we move on to being in the flow, and then we move on to connecting with others, and surrendering and letting it go).

Lynne Twist, the author of *The Soul of Money* looked at various aspects of the economy. She shared that we can give soul to money, that what is happening right now with this economy is making us find ways of collaborating with each other, and that it's useless pointing the finger at the old system, because it has served its purpose. Commitment drives you, and life works through you – this is exactly how it feels.

What I'm seeing, as things unfold, is that when you allow life to flow through you it directs you to some unexpected places, and into meeting unexpected people, and your team shows up, and the money shows up, and everything just starts to make sense, and it feels blissful. I'm very thankful for having been here tonight, for having witnessed it and for now being able to share it with you.

COMMIT TO SOMETHING BIGGER THAN YOURSELF

Something they emphasised more than once is the importance of aiming for something bigger than ourselves, of *making a commitment* to something bigger than ourselves. For me, for example, my commitment is to getting the book out, but not just for the sake of getting the book out, but because it can inspire millions of people who have lost their jobs, who are scared or who want to make a juicier living.

Now this is all giving me the power to move things at lightning speed. This is why things are happening so fast right now, why this book is becoming possible in such a short space of time; why it's felt so easy to put together, when actually the process is not easy, but it feels to me like nothing. I feel like I'm carried with the flow of it all, by that river to my destination, and I wish the experience for everyone. If we let go of those oars, and you just allow it, then it unfolds for you. Yes, I know it's hard because fear rears its head – we think there's not enough money, for example – but when you start accepting that there *is* enough money, and it'll be provided along the way, then things really shift, and I needed to hear that again right now. It's for this reason that we participate in seminars.

I WAS A SHOPAHOLIC

Another interesting thing I heard at the conference was how spending money can be a way of comforting yourself when you feel lonely etc. In other words, we buy ourselves material things to compensate for lack of fulfilment, and this is, frankly, the state I was in for the six months I was in my last job. I've never spent so much more than I needed to! Those spending sprees were the only times when I felt connected. Sad to say, but that was the reality of it. The only time during the week when I would finally feel good and have a bit relief from the pressure I felt about everything, was for those five minutes (or an hour, or whatever it was) when I bought umpteen clothes. I would feel satisfied by those purchases – I would feel good – and I thought that that was a natural way of life in London, from what I had heard from some negative source before I moved here. I didn't fully listen to or think about this opinion, and I just moved to the UK. Yes, I still love shopping and putting on nice clothes, but it's not coming from emptiness.

BE GRATEFUL AND HAPPINESS FOLLOWS

Tonight I went to get more of my Master Cleanse supplies from Whole Foods (I'm on Day 5), and then I got some beautiful red flowers for my room. They're so beautiful, and I cannot wait to have them on my desk – my career area – where I need to put some water, according to the feng shui. I have to remember: metal and water are the important elements in the career area, which corresponds to the north of my room, which is where I have my desk. Yes, I'll place these beautiful red flowers there. They'll go wonderfully with the theme of the room, putting it all in harmony, and making me even more grateful, and you know they what they say: gratefulness is the true gift of life. What brings even more happiness is being present to what you have, just the way it is right now. This is one of the most beautiful things. At one point I used to wake up and say five things that I was grateful for, and do the same thing at bedtime. Since then, having formed that habit over 100 days, I just spontaneously do it all day, at any time, for small, beautiful things, or big things that happen; I give thanks and feel gratitude. The funny thing about happiness is that it's not once you're happy that you start being grateful: be grateful and then you become happy!

Here is one of my favourite quotes: *'It is not happiness that makes us grateful but gratefulness that makes us happy.'*
– Br. David Steindl-Rast

I LOST MY JOB AND I LIKED IT

I can't get Katy Perry's song, 'I Kissed a Girl and I Liked It', out of my head. It's a very popular and catchy tune, and it's been going round and round in my mind, only the words come out as, 'I lost my job and I liked it', instead. It lifts me up just singing it. Since I woke this morning I have been thinking I should use this version as the title of my book. It's the sort of heading you might use for a blog posting. I'm also considering downloading all the lyrics of this song and modifying them to fit my situation, and then recording it and making a video to go along with it, and then putting that on YouTube (appropriately titled!), with the intention of it going viral. ...Get the word out there, and if people want more, then there is a book! It's a cool, fun thing to do, and I get a creative buzz just thinking about it. Yes, it's no coincidence that that song was stuck in my mind since Day 1. The fact that it is playful and fun is no bad thing, because it might help people feel a bit more 'chilled' about losing their jobs! Singing is a great practice too to shift energies, isn't it?

DOWNSTREAM

We can go either upstream or downstream, as Jerry and Esther Hicks' books suggest. I really enjoy reading their stuff. I see them as an important source of information on the Law of Attraction. I particularly love their books *Ask and It Is Given* and *The Astonishing Power of Emotions*. They describe going upstream as hard work, a struggle against resistance, requiring determination and a I-will-get-there-no-matter-what attitude. Going downstream, by contrast, means accepting things as they are, going with the flow, enjoying the ride and focusing primarily on feeling good. This is how I feel right now. I have allowed things to happen since the beginning of this book, since I was fired. I thought, 'I'll take that ride!' and the ride keeps on getting better!

VIRAL LYRICS?

I just worked on the song and it's definitely right. I love it. Both the book and the song will be called 'I Lost My Job and I Liked It'.

This was never the way I planned
Not my intention
I got so bored, pen in hand

Hit by recession
It's not what I'm used to
Just wanna try move on
I'm curious anew
Goodbye depression

I lost my job and I liked it
The taste of this crazy crisis
I lost my job, can't deny it
And now my dream job, I'll find it
It felt so good
It felt so right
Don't mean I'll get drunk tonight
I lost my job and I liked it
I liked it

Now, I don't really feel the same
It's getting better
It's an experimental game
And second nature
It's not what I'm used to
Not how I would behave
My heart no more confused
Can't now betray

I lost my job and I liked it
The taste of this crazy crisis
I lost my job, can't deny it
And now my dream job, I'll find it
It felt so good
It felt so right
Don't mean I'll get drunk tonight
I lost my job and I liked it
I liked it

My life is now so magical
No fuss, no boss, it's possible
High road to bliss so viable
So good you should try it
And now I feel magnificent

I lost my job and I liked it
The taste of this crazy crisis
I lost my job, can't deny it
And now my dream job, I'll find it
It felt so good
It felt so right
Don't mean I'll get drunk tonight
I lost my job and I liked it
I liked it

How fun is that! I'm thinking of recording it in a studio! With pictures and a video in mind, I've looked at how Katy Perry – the writer and singer of the original version of the song, 'I Kissed a Girl and I Liked It' – presents herself. I really liked her shots – superficially innocent yet open to interpretation – so I think I will do something similar, although, instead of having a watermelon, why not have an avocado? Combined with my previous ideas, we should then have the cover of the book!

ANTICIPATING JACK

I am looking forward to meeting Jack Latimer, the student photographer. I admire his work. He is young but talented, and I believe together we'll do something great around London, a city with which he is very familiar (unlike my friend Steven Martine). On Monday afternoon Jack and I will chew over the various ideas. I know that he's thrilled to be part of this, and is aware of what an opportunity it might be for him. It's wonderful to think that through the process of following the Law of Attraction and writing this book I might be able to help somebody so gifted, and, similarly, to help all the others who form part of the team needed to take this book to the world.

ME, SINGING?

11.11. I love it. It's Saturday morning and I'm on my way to the hairdresser and I'm singing my song: 'I lost my job and I liked it.' This is definitely the right title for the book. I'm going to keep this secret for now, and I'm going to contact Capitol Records (the company behind Katy Perry's song), because I would like to do this properly and get their approval. I'm really having fun with this! I am totally in the flow. Wow! I cannot believe I said that I was going to sing it. I cannot sing. I am a horrible singer! What possessed me? Gee, I am on fire! Can I sing it?

ON A HIGH AFTER A ROOF-TOP PARTY

I had a great time last night at the roof garden singles' party I organised. About 150 people showed up. I'm definitely going to have my book launch at the same venue. It'll be fabulous up there, especially at the end of April when we are likely to have a bit of sun. It's a top-notch club, really well run – you can tell that Sir Richard Branson is behind it. This morning, after that fun evening, I'm just so excited about life. I had very little sleep. I can't stay in bed in the morning; my flatmates find this very funny, for some reason. So, anyway, a couple of thoughts this morning… One is that I definitely want to keep on asking because, as I have said many times, the flow seems to increase when I do more asking.

MUSIC

I've received an email from my friend Daniel. I had sent him the lyrics of the song and the idea for the book title, and he loved both, so, with his approval, it's definitely a go. He's also sent me the sheet music for the song, which I hadn't thought of, so I could have somebody playing guitar or something. Otherwise, I could download the karaoke version, as Lili Roquelin (a singer and one of the participants in the '100-Day Reality Challenge' http://www.youtube.com/user/liliroquelin) recommended, and just sing the lyrics over it.

THE SPEED OF THINGS

All this is happening really fast, I admit, but, even so, I'm surprised that people are quite so astounded at the speed at which it is coming together – 'What? You're writing a book in four weeks? I mean, how do you do that? How is that possible?' Well, I'm simply allowing it to happen, so a complex process is becoming effortless as things just fall into place. To tell you the truth, if I had sat down and analysed this at the outset, and considered in detail all the steps that were needed to get a book out, I probably would have felt discouraged. Instead, I had a vision, and I allowed it to unfold, only ever seeing a few steps ahead and taking one action at a time, as guided by inspiration.

IDEAS FOR THE SONG VIDEO

I'm now thinking that instead of shooting a video for the song, maybe I should just edit together some excerpts from the videos in my 'From job loss to dream job' playlist (http://www.youtube.com/view_play_list?p=C9EFCF9BF0D4DB7A) with some pictures from the photo shoot I shall be doing this week. I think that could work really well, and would not involve that much extra work – editing, yes, but no further recording. Besides I want the video, like the book, to be authentic and fun!

APPLYING THE LAW OF ATTRACTION TO TRAINS AND PARKING SPOTS

Something that often makes me laugh is when friends say, 'The tube train only arrives at Kensington High Street every 15 minutes, and so you might have to wait.' I expect the train to be there when I arrive, and it generally is, and, funnily enough, this is exactly what happens when I want to attract anything else. When I lived in the River North district of central Chicago I didn't have a private parking space and had to use a public one. I would expect to find an empty parking spot when I needed it, and it would always be there, right in front of where I lived, and people would be amazed, not least the doorman, with whom I had a running joke on the subject. So try the Law of Attraction on small things like this. Start with a parking spot instead of £10,000 (or other big things you might have doubts about). I think you'll be surprised by how well the Law of Attraction works, and by how quickly you start to build confidence.

ASKING FOR GUIDANCE AGAIN

I want to ask Life to enlighten me and provide with some new business ideas related to this book. For example, maybe I should set up a community?

EVERY CLOUD…

An apparent disaster with my iPhone has turned out to be a bit of a blessing. I was transferring data between my iPhone and my new iMac and screwed up all the contacts, ending up with 2,000 emails in my phone and no phone numbers! '*Merde alors*!' I thought. Last night, therefore, I started going through each email, one by one, intending to delete them. It turned out to be a great opportunity to refresh my memory about all the people I have been on touch with, and to consider who might be able help me with the promotion of the book, or just in general. For example, I came across emails from Harpo Studios – *The Oprah Winfrey Show* – from the time they did a minute on 18 participants of the '100-Day Reality Challenge' to be featured in their Law-of-Attraction show. In the end they did not use that video, but I kept those contacts! Without the phone disaster it's highly unlikely I would have found them because I hadn't labelled or indexed the emails.

AUDIO BOOKS

I just purchased, from Amazon, the audio-book version of *The Soul of Money* by Lynne Twist. I can listen to it when I'm on public transport, and I think it's going to be a great book and very insightful. This reminds me that I should probably produce an audio version of this book too. I like to buy audio books, and particularly appreciated them when I had a car – I transformed it into a library. That was great. I miss those Chicago traffic jams just for that reason! So inspiring. Now I have the tube.

THE LAYOUT OF THE BOOK BECOMES CLEARER

This is Day 8 of the Master Cleanse. I was just looking at a nicely presented, colour-coded IBM report I found on the Internet called 'The Enterprise of the Future'. The title caught my eye because I want to have a general overview of how companies might evolve in the future. As I was reading through it, my attention was caught by the title page for Chapter 2. There's something about the layout that I really like, and so the appearance of my series of books is becoming clearer to me. I'm now considering using really clean lines, with a picture of me at the top of the front cover. The bottom of it will have a distinctive colour, and each book of the series will be colour-coded. The present book is about finding a job. I'll choose a colour for it, and I can work through all the colours of the rainbow for subsequent titles. I think the series will look awesome! Again, this feels like the Law of Attraction at work – another thing kicking in. …And it really kicked it, because when I looked at the picture, I just couldn't tear my eyes away from it. Such a strong feeling really calls for action.

I haven't yet found anybody to do the cover, but I can give it a shot myself, and do some mock-ups on Photoshop. I used to have an old website called MpowerU.com, which is no longer online, but on which I grouped information according to colour. Money was represented by green, and red was for love, blue for peace etc. So I'm used to the concept of colour-coding, and can easily get back into it. I can already see my colour-coded books all lined up on a shelf, a Law-of-Attraction rainbow!

You know what? I even like the typeface the IBM report is set in, and how the titles are laid out, and how it's written – there's something I really like about the cleanness, the aesthetics – so I think I've even found the format for the interior of my book. I must identify the font!

THE LAWS OF MANIFESTATION

I just received a beautiful book and postcard as a gift from someone who saw one of my videos on YouTube, and this person says:

> *Dear Lilou,*
> *I completed reading the Laws of Manifestation book and*
> *am sending it along to you, as I said. I believe you will truly*
> *enjoy many additional insights offered from the experiences*
> *of the author on manifestation. It truly is an exciting time*
> *as we uncover, rediscover, and open ourselves up to our*
> *greatest potential. Thank you for allowing me to share with*
> *you and play observer. Now I'm stepping up, my co-creator.*
> *Love,*
> *Sarah*

And this book is *The Laws of Manifestation* by David Spangler. I received an email from Sarah a week ago saying that she absolutely loved the book and wanted to send it to me. I am very much looking forward to reading it – it's exciting! What a lovely and generous gesture it was to send it to me!

THE MINUTE OF REAL NEWS

I'm going to make a one-minute news video for YouTube. Since that breakthrough a couple of weeks ago I've been reading the news every day, and there are a couple of news items that I could share in one minute with my YouTube audience. I'll probably call it something like 'The Minute Of Real News'. I thought I would share with you the contents of my first such news video, the first item of which is that '*The Bank of England will create £150 billion of new money, 75 billion of which will be used within the next three months to help the UK recover and to help people spend more*'. This contrasts with a long history of managing things to prevent inflation! They don't have a clue about what the effect of injecting all this new money will be. The Bank of England hasn't done anything like this for the entire 315 years of its existence – this is how the British are reacting!

'*Japanese exports declined by 45% in the first two weeks of February.*' As you know, Japan is a big exporter, so a drop of 45% will have a huge impact on their economy, and God knows what it's going to like there, but it looks pretty bad.

In the last six months, there have been millions and millions of job losses. In the USA in February alone, '*650,000 jobs were lost and in 2008 5.4 million US homeowners – that's one in eight – fell behind with their loan repayments.*' You can imagine that's billions of dollars unpaid, and no money coming in to the lenders.

These are just a few of the news items. I'm not doing this to make people depressed – my videos are definitely meant to inspire, but I also believe that it's very important to be aware of what's happening. Since that breakthrough I find myself getting a lot of power from taking the facts and figures on board, instead of putting myself in a bubble and pretending that everything is perfect.

MEETING JACK

I just met Jack, the photographer, at the local Starbucks. He's definitely the person I need for this – clever and creative – and he's definitely passionate about what he is doing. We discussed the whole schedule. We're going to do the shoot on Thursday using his ideas for a dramatic background. We're going to do some shots in the morning around Bank Station in the middle of the City – big city shots at rush hour… The idea is to have a chaotic rush-hour backdrop for some of my promotional shots, and maybe one of them will end up being the cover… I don't know. Then we'll do the indoor pictures at my home in the afternoon. It's fabulous. I'm super-happy to have attracted him as the photographer for this. I have a really good feeling about it. He has some great ideas! Now I understand why it didn't work out with Steven; Jack knows London, and is young and creative… new blood, new juice. He's from Brixton originally, so he's definitely making suggestions that Steven couldn't have, even though Steven is a supremely talented photographer. This is all great!

Now, as far as the indoor shots are concerned… Well, I very much like Katy Perry's photos on her website. She has a lot of innocent, fresh, playful, fun, fresh expressions which I will try to use both outside, against the dramatic backdrop, and inside, and we'll do some shots with me using my iPhone, and all kinds of things, so that I can use them for the video. I'm so excited! It's so much fun to be in this flow.

WORKING TOGETHER

Things are really coming together. I'm receiving the transcriptions from Margie in the Philippines; she's doing a great job! I'm receiving the edited text from Eric in Scotland. I posted the CCOR events online and I've got a couple of participants already. It's funny how the flow of money is working. It's OK. I need to pay Eric and Margie, and also secure a house for the CCOR weekend, but for some reason I feel fully supported by Life. Although fears pop up now and again, I keep cancelling those negative thoughts and re-creating them, moment by moment.

Right now, I'm preparing all the memos and the mp3s of my iPhone recordings so that Margie can type them up. It's amazing how the whole chain is coming together and being orchestrated! I love it. This is a relatively new feeling for me; I used to do things on my own. Again I must express my gratitude for the experience I had with the company I was working for, because, without that, I don't think I could have done the job I'm doing now, and I am so much more appreciative of the fact that I'm living with passion and on purpose after my previous work experience. I was once told that we learn more from contrasts, from those hard moments in our lives; they help us find what we really want, what is really important. I certainly believe this to be true. Why not be grateful for these contrasts then? Why not be grateful for things that don't go our way? For it being hard? Properly interpreted, they will get us closer to where we truly want to go!

ASK AND IT IS GIVEN

I just received an email from Camilla in Norway:

Hi Lilou,
I watch your videos every time you put them on YouTube.
I get so inspired and I know you're going to become the
next Oprah. I look forward to the book you're writing and of

*course, I'm buying it. Can I ask you for some advice if you
have the time? I love fashion. I know that that's my passion
in life but I want to work from home with my passion. How
do you think I can start to reach my goal? Do you have any
advice or do you know someone in CCOR who have the
same goal I can ask for advice?*
Camilla from Norway

Well, Camilla…

(I just sent her an email back but basically, she's going to love this book!)

Camilla, you're going to read this book. You said you're going to buy it. Now, you're going to see why I sent you that email!

Yes, a lot of people in CCOR (including, of course, myself!) are going after their passion, so it is the sort of community where you will find the kind of support illustrated by this little exchange. I'll definitely do a video on this subject. In my reply to Camilla I let her know that I'll probably call that video 'Ask and It Is Given', because I think she's very much in a situation where she would need to ask for guidance, and need to remember to keep asking for it. The importance of this is illustrated by what happened to me the other day, when I felt that I was not asking enough and, consequently, not creating a strong flow and continuing to dream sufficiently. Yes, ask, because it's really life-enhancing!

REMEMBRANCE OF THINGS PAST: MY JOURNALING HISTORY

I've just realised that I've been writing journals since I was seven years old. I grew up in France but I lived with my parents in Scottsdale, Arizona, from the age of six until eight, and, when I was about seven,

I received my first little journal as a gift from an American friend. It was pink with little teddy bears and blue hearts on it, and had a pink satin ribbon to secure it. I took it with me back to France and it really helped me cope with the transition. It was a very hard time because when you're eight you make such good friends, and I felt that my roots were being torn off. The journal helped me express all that. For some reason I called it 'Jimmy'. I don't know where that name came from, but that was 'his' name, and I would confide in him, saying everything that was going through my mind. Thinking back, I had always wanted a big brother, so that is probably why my journal buddy became Jimmy. Someone I could talk to and learn from.

My parents divorced when I was 12, and my journal helped a lot then too. I felt isolated – that nobody could understand me – because, in the very Catholic school I went to, there were few, if any, other kids in my position. My journal was the thing that got me through this, and helped me to feel connected again, and my many subsequent journals have continued to help me deal with various issues over the years. I have kept them all. Anyway, by the time it came to CCOR and the '100-Day Reality Challenge', the way they worked – with journaling and video blogs – seemed natural to me. I had always said to myself that those journals would one day come in handy, and I always had the feeling that I would publish them, and it's funny that I'm just realising now that my first book is actually a diary, so it's coming true – it's happening! I have a big smile on my face now. I can see how my whole journey has been unfolding and will continue to unfold.

HOME AT LAST

2.11! 2.11 p.m., and it's raining. I was just listening to 'Amazing Grace'. I'm so grateful for where I live. I feel so good. I just stepped into Henrik's room and let him know how grateful I am for the house and for having him and Giada as flatmates, because it's really amazing.

Every day, I think, 'Wow! I live here. I love it.' When you have lived through something that you didn't particularly like, it's amazing how much more grateful you are for things that really correspond to what you have always been asking for. I feel now that I can settle properly for the first time. I've moved around so often. Now, though, I feel at home in England – in London – and it really feels good to buy furniture and settle in, so it's definitely a big new chapter in my life.

A PRESENT FOR DAD

One of the things I want to do soon is to get someone to type up my dad's *The Art of Cooking Zen* manuscript. I'll find somebody to turn it into really good French, and possibly even translate it into English, and I'll publish it for him as a gift. I cannot wait for this moment because, unfortunately, he has done many things in his life but did not finish this one. He would just love it! It's something he's been speaking about for so long (that and writing his memoirs, which he is doing now – he says this is bringing back a lot of emotions and that it has been therapeutic) and it's within my capacity to give him that unexpected help and make sure he gets that book. It's going to be such a precious gift and a beautiful thing. I cannot wait!

DID I JUST MANIFEST A FREE RIVER CRUISE?

I just received an email from Bob Watson back in the USA. Bob is like my American dad. I've known him since I moved back to the USA in 2000. I used to work for a tour operator and I would help him with his groups of people going to France. Bob was then my first client when I started my website and Internet marketing company after September 11, 2001. He's booked a cruise from the April the 6th to the 13th, leaving from Amsterdam and passing through Holland and Belgium. Twenty-nine travel agents will be going on it. He would like me to run the seminars on the boat. Basically, what it amounts to is a free cruise for an entire week, on a beautiful luxury ship, something for which one would normally pay $2,000, so I'm very, very tempted to go. I called my mom to see if she'd like to come along. She can't make it, but I'm thinking of taking my dad, so I'm going to contact him tomorrow. I also have to check with CreateSpace if I can receive a proof copy of the book before I go on the cruise, but that sounds feasible. The date coincides with the final stages of the book, when it should largely be out of my hands, and yet it falls before the CCOR event and the book launch, so it could work well. Besides, the ship is fully equipped: wi-fi, computers, a fitness centre, premium local wines flowing every day... and it's all-inclusive! What more could I ask for?

BATTLING THOUGHTS OF SCARCITY AGAIN

It's unbelievable how strongly our thoughts of scarcity are anchored in our minds! Gee, they just keep on popping up, and the thing is that when you don't catch them early enough they can snowball, as one negative thought attracts another. I've got to stop this and cancel those thoughts, and re-create something more positive, because here I am now starting to freak out: 'Oh yeah, but what if the CCOR weekend doesn't sell? What if then I'm stuck with the house? What if I don't even have ten participants? What if I don't make any sales on the book?' And so on and so forth. Because of this mindset, I'm definitely not in a good place to make the right decision regarding the cruise right now. But I will make a decision by Monday. I must give this some thought or, should I say, thoughts... some positive thoughts! That's probably what's missing here. So I am declaring the possibility of being guided, and finding abundance in my mind and re-creating my thoughts in order to have a mindset of abundance. I'm now on my way to the gym.

NERVES

I can't believe I'm actually nervous about that photo shoot. I keep thinking about it. It's on Thursday. Right now, it's Tuesday night. It's only a photo shoot. What's wrong with me? We're going to do this in London and then at home. It's as if I fear that I'm not going to get it, or that it's not going to be great, or... so I have to cancel these thoughts. I'm creating the possibility that it'll be a perfect day for this shoot, and that the pictures will come out spectacularly well. It's even going to be hard to choose between them, because all of them are going to be awesome, but, definitely, out of all of those, the picture for the cover will stand out clearly, and the cover will be great!

I'm creating a magnificent day for tomorrow, productive, and in-the-flow, such that time will slow down. I have time to do many things well, focusing on each in turn, and I look forward to tomorrow. Big days ahead!

NEVER SATISFIED? KEEP ON ASKING.

I wonder why it's so difficult to ask for more sometimes. You see that the flow is cooperating and your response is, 'Yeah, I'm not asking for as much now. What more can I possibly ask for?' I don't think we've been raised to ask for a lot of things. When I was growing up I was always scolded for asking for too much. So now I have to rewire and retrain myself, to ask more of Life, to ask of myself too, and it's interesting how much I'm struggling. I would have thought that I'd be the last person to struggle with this kind of stuff, being someone who is, according to my mother 'never satisfied', but now that I can see that this is of the essence, I'm wondering what I can ask for next!

MORE THOUGHTS ABOUT THE NEWS

I'm on my way to the Calumet store, which specialises in photographic equipment. I'm looking for a white backdrop, potentially to do some more professional-looking videos from home. I know they have a great specialist who'll be able to advise me on both the background and the lighting I would need to give my videos that extra touch, so I can take them that bit further. I intend to do more Internet interviews and videos such as the 'Minute of Real News'. To judge by people's comments, they really appreciate having that kind of worldwide news on the current situation. Again, I feel the need to emphasises the fact that I'm not doing this to focus on the negative. No, we are currently experiencing an economy that it is about to undergo major transformation: we're in the catalytic stages. Big changes are underway, millions of people are losing their jobs, there is bad news pretty much every day, and this might last for another four or five years. Even Warren Buffett said yesterday in the New York Post that he's expecting it to be at least five years. He's comparing it to Pearl Harbor – to a world war! – but this is what we have to face.

CO-CREATING

We must get real, and see millions of jobs are being lost everywhere. This is the truth. It doesn't have to make us depressed. We have to find the power, our own power in this... in what role we're going to play in this, because we all have a unique role and this is the time for us to wake up. All of us.

I'm very grateful to be here in Europe now, and to be working on this project, and maybe helping others to open their eyes to the reality and yet understand that they are not powerless. We have the power to co-create our reality – not just create but co-create. We can't do it on our own, and we're never, frankly, doing it on our own. We do it with other people, with Source if we're spiritual, and with God if we are religious, but we're never on our own. So this is the kind of stuff that it's time for us to realise, and to use to the fullest extent in order to face this economy, to face what's happening now, and I have strong faith in human potential. I've always been interested in this subject. What does it take to be an extraordinary human being? That's something that's always fascinated me, and I know that this is the time for me to find that 'extraordinariness' in myself, and become a leader and to empower and inspire those who want to be empowered and inspired – to do something and make their lives happen. This is the time, guys. This is the time.

THE JUICE FLOWS

It's now nearly a month since I lost my job. I am really enjoying how all this is progressing and the many things that have happened. The speed of it all testifies to the power of the Law of Attraction when you really start tapping into it and being in the flow. It's beyond what you can imagine, but that's what makes it so juicy. God, I love that word, 'juicy'. Ha, like an orange that you squeeze. That's life – full of juice, full of vitamins and greatness.

TRYING TRIPODS AND LUGGING LIGHTS

I just got back from the Calumet store. In the course of conversation, I discovered that Calumet rents out photographic equipment, so I asked if I could rent a whiite backdrop to try it out. We can use it for the pictures and I can try doing some of my videos with it. So that's two things I could try out. I'm going to use it for the cover and promotional pictures shot in my home. I called Jack to see if he needed any other gear, since he might not be able to afford the greatest equipment. I wanted to transform my home into a studio, and I ended up renting a whole bunch of tripods and lights, which I had to encourage him to take so that he could give full rein to his talents. You see, I really want to help Jack.

He is a 22-year-old student. I was blessed to receive, at the beginning of my career, a great deal of help from mentors, clients and various others. They believed in me. I am now sending the elevator back down! It feels great!

I am looking forward to the shoot tomorrow!

I recorded my one-minute video of the real news, 'The Minute of Real News', and I even bought www.minuteofrealnews.com. I'll see what I do with that. I also recorded my Day 56 of my '100-Day Reality Challenge' today to update everyone, and I feel as prepared as I could be for tomorrow.

THE MASCHA SHOCK

It's 3.11 p.m. I received an email from Mascha. She can't come to the CCOR meeting that's taking place in London in April. All of a sudden all those negative thoughts rushed back, because it's originally because of the email that I received from her that this whole idea of the London event started. My mind immediately jumped to: 'Oh no. Nobody's registering. I only have two participants so far. Maybe, this is not a good idea. Maybe I shouldn't have rented the house and everything!' Now I'm committed, so I have that whole house booked for the weekend of 24 April. But I believe there is no such thing as coincidence and I want to interpret this from the point of view that that there's a reason things have happened like this... There's a reason for me having that house on that weekend and attracting participants. Ideally I would like to attract 30 participants to come over to London. My mind immediately says, 'Oh, there's a financial crisis. People cannot afford it.' But this is what I'm then going to attract. Come to think of it, this is what I have been attracting, because this is the background thought that I had! So now it's about fully creating the possibility of having 30 participants come to London, and getting new ideas on how to promote it and how to share it with people, encouraging everyone to come. Mascha may have cancelled, but I'm sure it's for the best. I'm sure something good is going to come out of this now that I have this whole mansion for that weekend. I'm going to make the most of it, and I'm sure what will come out of it will be spectacular.

THE END OF THE CLEANSE

Today's Day 10 of the Master Cleanse, so tomorrow I'm going to drink only freshly squeezed orange juice to get my digestive system slowly to start working again. I just bought some juicy organic oranges and some avocados for the photo shoot. I feel very, very good. I had great energy levels during the entire Master Cleanse. I was able to go to the gym on a regular basis, and do everything that I needed to do (and I've been very busy running around). So, yeah, it's been great as usual. I love doing it once in a while. You can do it for up to 40 days, but I think that might be a bit much. One day, maybe, I'll do it... For now, I look forward to rediscovering the joy of eating, and especially of eating greens. Once your body is clean like that – squeaky clean – you crave greens and living foods.

NOT TELLING MOM

I haven't told my mom yet that I was writing a book and pursuing my passion. I have to say I'm a bit scared to tell her and experience her reaction. However, yesterday I spoke with her on the phone, and I did mention that I was organising a weekend, and she said that she had gleaned that from my videos, so I guess my message is so out there that even my mom knows what I'm up to, but she didn't mention anything about the book. I'm not sure when and how I'm going to tell her. I want to make sure I'm in a position where everything is fully aligned and rolling before I tell. I think this moment will come soon. I just need to get it a bit further off the ground, and protect this dream of mine until I can safely let her know the full extent of it.

PHOTO SHOOT HIGHS AND LOWS

8.11. Yes, 8.11 a.m. on this day of the photo shoot for the cover of the book. I'm in the middle of the City at rush hour. I'm just walking from Monument Tube Station to Bank Station to meet Jack, and there's something that is just… moving me emotionally. I don't know what it is in the air that I feel today. It's not that I want to cry, but I'm very moved; at the same time, inspired; at the same time, touched, but kind of sad about what's happening in the world. I can feel it in the air here.

I look forward to today. I'm creating the possibility of an awesome photo shoot, inspiring, that will turn out amazing. I also intend to be playful, to have fun. OK, time to go and take the pictures.

So we just did some shooting and it really came out great I think! In the City, in the tube station, on the Waterloo Bridge, and on the lions of Trafalgar Square. Right now, however, I'm going through a patch when I'm having more than a little bit of a hard time. I'm find the indoor shoot very difficult. I got myself imprisoned in negative thoughts, until the moment I said, 'Let's have a break here, because I can't do this. It's not working.' I just ate half an avocado, because I felt that my body needed more vitamins today than the orange could provide. While Jack is away, I'm doing a bit of reiki, and re-centring myself – refocusing. I *so* much want to get this right – and I am sobbing now. I think my perfectionist streak is getting in the way. I'm not allowing myself to just be with the flow, and enjoy the moment. I'm putting too much pressure on myself right now, so I have to release that. I have to re-create something that will go well. I'll have some great indoor shots. It's interesting how just one negative thought can lead to another and, before you know it, you're off at the bottom of that rabbit hole! How deep do you want to dig that rabbit hole?

After that little break I was able to shift that negative energy and continue with the photo shoot, and I believe we have the cover of the book, so that's very satisfying! I particularly like the one where I'm holding the book in front of me, and I'm holding an open journal in front of me (full of text, as if I have been scrawling away all day) and in the other hand I'm holding an avocado. I'm playing with those two elements as I'm very much into eating healthily eating and, of course, this is a diary – my journal.

TELLING DAD

I finally got my dad on the phone (he called), and I told him my news, and I was really open because I thought he was going to be supportive. He has been away for three months travelling in Vietnam, Laos and Cambodia, so I had to update him on the situation. I said, 'Listen, I've lost my job, but I'm writing a book.' His reaction took me by surprise. With hindsight, I should perhaps have kept things to myself but I really wanted to tell him.

He said, 'Yeah, but you've got to keep your feet on the ground and be realistic about all this.'

'Yeah, Dad,' I replied, 'I'm really considering everything, and I'm working hard at it and things are coming together.'

This is a tricky situation. It's not about proving things to him, but I *do* have a plan. In a way he's right, though. In the past I never put 100% into making things happen, and the outside world – my parents – can only go on what they know of me. They are not fully aware of everything I'm doing now, so I don't think they realise how important this is to me (and, frankly, I hadn't realised myself until recently), and so Dad has to catch up. I cannot blame him for his response, but I am saddened by the idea that he's not supporting me right now. I'm sad that he's worried, which then adds to my worries.

So, Lilou, this is it! This is your time now – to realise your dreams, and tomorrow is a big day and you can do it.

PSYCHED FOR SUCCESS

It's Friday the 13th, and I've got a couple of minor meetings, and then an important one in the afternoon, and I'm going to give it my all. I'm going to give of my best. More than ever, I am enthused and passionate and my dream is happening. I'm going to breathe deeply, in and out, and allow all the greatness to come to fruition.

THE RHYTHM OF MONEY

Yesterday I listened to *The Soul of Money* by Lynne Twist. There's this sentence in track number one that got stuck in my mind: money needs to flow. It's like energy. Money needs to flow in and out, and I'm getting worried, particularly now, seeing the money going out, to pay for this and that, when I have no guarantee that this project is going to be a success – I'm putting all my money into it! It was that pressure that I was feeling from the photo shoots. Not only did I rent equipment, but I also hired someone to do the pictures. It adds up. Part of me was thinking, 'There's this money going out, but by allowing it to go out, and involve and help others, it will flow back'. So I'm practising this. I'm learning, and, yeah, it's one of the challenges I'm facing at the moment. I must remember that it's not about me. The focus is on helping others here, helping people to get through these hard times. I want to help. This is where my strength lies, and where the motivation to grow and to continue with this process comes from.

I'm creating a nice, relaxing evening. I'm going to switch the computer off and listen to some good music, watch a movie, or read a book. I'll light some candles, and maybe have a little bath and just relax... breathe, and be in the present moment. Then my intention is to have a beautiful deep sleep and wake up tomorrow morning around 8 o'clock fully refreshed and full of beautiful energy, ready to go out.

Tomorrow will be a day of playfulness, of being fully myself, of being 100% on purpose, of enjoying the process, of opening myself up, of sharing and conquering.

SUPPORTIVE AND INSIGHTFUL COMMENTS

Yes, it's possible to shift energy very fast. I just felt inspired to go to my Day 35 video (http://www.youtube.com/watch?v=hwshffMkZPw) in which I announced the loss of my job. People have posted some wonderful comments on it, that are really inspiring me and pumping me up. There is one from klady3818 (that's her YouTube name):

Lilou, you are an inspiration. I too have lost my job recently and I have just been spinning my wheels. I hope that you will continue to post your personal progress so that I can follow your inspirational lead. You are someone that I do admire for being so open and candid. Please keep going!

These kinds of messages definitely confirm that I'm on the right path, and that I should continue my journey!

Marla from California (YouTube username Marlamartenson) also wrote a comment on my Day 35, Season 11 video. She is the author of *Excuse Me, Your Soul Mate Is Waiting* (http://www.cocreatingourreality. com/group/excusemeyoursoulmateiswaiting) which is about using the Law of Attraction to attract your soul mate. I interviewed her in Chicago for my show, *Live a Juicy Life*. She writes:

Great video, thanks for sharing! So many people are in your position and need some positive reassurance.

And here's another one, this time from 'Clarion13' (http://www. youtube.com/clarion13). Clarisse has been a '100-Day Reality Challenge' participant since 2006. She comments:

WOW thank you for this!!! Yes, it is a JUICY ride this season! Mine is, too! I am finding that it is MUCH easier to stay in the flow than ever before, even when I get down I get RIGHT BACK UP and that is a big thing for me! I am finding that the positive flow is becoming a way of life for me, just as you are. I am soooo excited to see what happens next!

Yeah, it's so true what Clarisse is saying here. It is really like that. The more you practise, the more you are in this constant flow. Yes, there are some down times, but they don't last long. Life flows through you easily and effortlessly as you learn to allow it to, and get out of the way!

You start to know yourself as someone who can create anything that your heart desires, especially when you have the support of a community such as that. I thank God for my subscribers on YouTube, and the CCOR members. Again, I feel so grateful, because whenever I am down and read messages like the ones I just shared, I am lifted right back up!

To date I have received 41 comments on this video alone. Each of them is pure bliss. Sure, I do sometimes receive negative comments – my videos are public and can be viewed by anyone. But that is part of the fun, isn't it? I do sometimes wonder, though, why some viewers add nasty messages. My intentions are good, and my message is positive. I guess some people cannot quite tolerate people loving life. I know they will be ready some day, and I know that some of them are changing their minds about how the world works because of all the videos I put online, particularly when I demonstrate the before (declaration) and after (manifestation). Negative comments make me laugh now!

After reading those positive messages I felt inspired to go to the Co-Creating Our Reality website and have a look at my own page (http://

www.cocreatingourreality.com/profile/Lilou). I found myself looking at my music section where I had posted a declaration I did years ago. I played it (as anybody can do). It's a four-minutes declaration. I just listened to it, and I'm back in the flow again. I am now ready for a good sleep. I am peacefully inspired and will be carried by the soft rhythm of the dreams that will take me through the night. Hmm! Good night, Co-Creator.

THIRTEEN IS ANOTHER OF MY LUCKY NUMBERS!

Well, today is Friday the 13th of March. It's a big day today, and a big date in our family: Friday the 13th is lucky for us! Lots of big things have happened on Friday the 13th. My parents own a couple of restaurants in France, actually French-Mexican restaurants, if you can believe it! I was born in Santa Barbara, California, because my parents ran a French restaurant there. That's how I acquired dual citizenship. I then grew up back in France where my parents continued in the restaurant trade. Friday the 13th is a big day for us not least because that's when, in '87 – 22 years ago – they opened their restaurant in Nantes! It was the first Mexican restaurant there and was a real success, and so for us 13 is a great number. Add to that the facts that my mom grew up in a house of which the address was 13 rue des moulins, and I moved to Chicago from Miami (driving a rental truck and my car across the USA) on a Friday the 13th.

THE COVER SHOT

It's no surprise, then, that I feel particularly aligned and great today. This morning I was looking at all the pictures from yesterday's shoot, and I think I found the cover of the book. ☺ It's one of outdoor ones – picture 77, like my birth year, 1977. It's a shot where I'm looking to the side, there's a London bus passing by, and there are many people behind and to the side of me, busy reading their newspapers. It's the picture we took at 9 a.m. – rush hour – in the middle of the City. There's an alert and hopeful expression on my face, yet somehow thoughtful and fearful at the same time. There's confidence there too, and you can see dreams in my eyes, so I think this is it! Maybe it's too soon be certain, because there are also some great indoor shots, but I have to say this looks very, very promising. I really liked it, and, honestly, it jumped out at me (it gave me good vibrations) the first time I saw it. So, quite possibly, that's the cover shot right there! Oh, I'm so excited. It is coming together. This is so fulfilling. So fulfilling! I cannot express how full of life I feel – so juicy!

THE MAGNETISM OF SUPER-CONFIDENCE

Just as I learned to do in the Tony Robbins seminar about crossing hot coals, this morning I visualised receiving great news. I got into that kind of zone for 17 seconds, and then I started again for another 17 seconds. I cultivated that 'wow' feeling, fully celebrating – celebrating the fact that I have what I truly desire. That's the kind of peak energy you want to reach, a level that will attract the thing that you want so strongly that, when you turn up at an event, a meeting or an interview, you exude confidence, and have a magnetic charismatic presence. All your senses are awake. People go along with your intentions. They are drawn to your confidence and your certainty. So, needless to say, you are super-convincing, or, perhaps I should say, inviting. People want to be around you. They feel great about themselves, because you give permission to yourself to be fully who you are. This is one of the most powerful techniques I've come across. This, and the power move I was describing earlier. These two combined are rock solid. Although I found the rest of Tony's seminar entertaining, I have to say it was those two things that made it worthwhile.

A JUICY POSSIBILITY

So I have registered for the London Book Fair on April 20th. It just occurred to me that there's a possibility of attracting a publisher there! The book will be written, and probably already online, and with its potential, its timeliness, and the Law of Attraction on my side, publishers could well recognise its merits, so I'm thinking that finding one is well within the bounds of possibility. Obviously there are pros and cons to this, but one of the great possibilities is that I could get a lump sum of money up front ('an advance on future sales') if they believe as much as I do in the success of this book. An even juicier possibility is that several publishers see its potential and they bid to get the book! LOL

Now, the London Book Fair is from the 20th to the 22nd of April, just before the CCOR weekend. I only have a few participants for the CCOR weekend so far. For some reason it's just not picking up. (Well, I know the reason – my thoughts have been less confident and positive than they could have been.)

PREPARED FOR A CELEBRATION

But then I have already rented this beautiful mansion in Hyde Park, and I think some other people will register. They're just taking their time, but now that I have this house for that weekend, I'm thinking there is no coincidence here. The house has a cost. I've paid a deposit for it, and I'm responsible for renting it for two days and two nights. It's a significant amount of money. I suppose it was fairly natural that I would start worrying: 'What if I cannot get enough participants to even cover its cost? I would have to pay for it and this is a time when I should be pragmatic…'. But, you know what? Do you know what, Co-Creator? Let's say that this house was meant to be available to celebrate amazing great news, such as a contract with a publisher. Then the entire weekend would be a celebration weekend, and have made this project possible. Yes, that's an opportunity to give back, and share. How cool is that! I'm on a high.

PLAYFULNESS IS LIFE-GIVING

This morning, Henrik told me about this video on http://blog.ted.
com/. A polar bear is just about to attack two huskies in the Arctic,
but the female husky has her tail up and starts playing, and it totally
shifts the energy of the scene. What could have turned out very
violent becomes a beautiful, friendly dance. It's a very moving video
and reminds me to play. What a difference a playful attitude can
make to some situations. So let's get our inner child out and have
fun! Play definitely boosts creativity. It leads to innovation, to new
ways of thinking. This thought is very inspiring to me at this moment.
Yes, I'm feeling inspired and empowered to be playful all afternoon,
and all weekend. What am I saying here? – All Life!

A NATURAL EXTENSION

I can see this book is turning into a series of books. I just don't see
myself stopping sharing my life like this. I've been doing it on video
for years, and now writing takes my sharing to a whole other level.
It gives a better picture of how thoughts come together, and how
we can attract the life we want in all aspects – with regard to money,
relationships, peace, business success, anything! I love doing this!

I have often heard: 'Find a job that you are passionate about.' Well,
I've been writing journals since I was a kid, and I just love journaling.
That's why I enjoy doing videos on the '100-Day Reality Challenge',
and that's why it's been of so much help to me since I started
participating in it. So why stop? If I can make a living and make a
difference at the same time – feel fully on purpose – then I cannot
ask for anything better. It's fantastic. I would do it anyway. It's an
extension of me. This comes so naturally.

I once heard of this person who loved TV soap operas. There are
many such programmes in the USA; I guess in Europe too. One day

she started to do summaries and reviews of all the soap operas she watched, to keep others up to date. She made an extraordinary living from it, and she just loved it: her job was watching soap operas, which she would do anyway. She also created a community based on this, where people would discuss the latest ups and downs of their favourite characters. She couldn't ask for anything better!

We all have things like that, that we love to make or do – things that are extensions of ourselves, such that our souls sing when we do them, all our senses are awake, and our creativity is heightened.

I do not think of myself as a gifted writer, but I do think I can open up and share my insights articulately. It's a natural process for me, something I love doing and I would do anyway. I don't mind sharing my private life. I love doing it actually. If the insights that I have can help others to have insights, then that's awesome, and I've done my job! I have found my dream job! ☺

BEING FREE AGAIN

I cannot believe that it took me so long (after all those seminars, all those books) to understand that it is in the power of the heart, in the living out of our passions, that true Self resides and can be expressed.

I have been encouraging people to live lives of passion and purpose, but I was not on purpose myself. Now I am.

I feel alive and at the top of the mountain. I thank Life, and myself, for allowing all this to unfold, as it has unfolded and is unfolding.

My ego was in the way before. My former boss told me: 'You are a rough diamond.' I feel now that the diamond is no longer rough; it is cut and polished. It feels fantastic.

Maybe the company I was working for was 'rough'. Maybe it was me. Perhaps I added 'roughness' to the experience. My insecurities probably created that. But I now realise that I needed that experience in order to learn from it. I had some big lessons to learn. And, ultimately, I needed to write this book.

My ego was holding me back. Previously I refused to let go that part of me, as I was afraid of losing my identity. I let my ego run the show. I was afraid of what I would discover about myself, but what I find is that I am beautiful, human, genuine, and a loving and generous person, and I want to work with my talents and those of others. I want to lead great projects. I want to give of myself every day, and I want to give hope and joy to people. Coming to this self-actualisation is precious. It is life-giving.

I am so grateful.

This journey has all been worthwhile. All the struggles, the failures, the hard work, have all been worth it.

I have the feeling of being on the top of the mountain already, with open arms, breathing that fresh air, and being free again.

TO BE CONTINUED…

AFTERWORD

I hope that you have enjoyed reading my 30-day Law-of-Attraction journey. Remember that you are the co-creator of your life. You can create anything that you heart desires! Follow your passion. It is in following your passion that true creativity, joy, and self-expression reside. It is a magnificent journey. Listen to your heart. It will guide you.

I believe in you and send you all my love.

I invite you – even urge you – to join me in helping the millions of people around the word who need support: our support.

ABOUT THE AUTHOR

Lilou's mission and vision is to help millions of people to live a joyful and fulfilled life.

Lilou was born in Santa Barbara, California, in August 1977, of French parents. She grew up in Nantes, France, and, after graduating from Oxford Brookes University (UK) and ESC La Rochelle (France) with a BA in European Business Studies, returned to the United States, where she lived from November 2000 to July 2008. She now lives in London.

Lilou Mace is a co-founder of the '100-Day Reality Challenge', a global community experiencing the magic and power of the Law of Attraction 100 days at a time.

From November 2001 until July 2008 Lilou was also the owner of 'Emotional Brands', a website design and online branding agency based in Chicago and Fort Lauderdale.

Lilou lived in Chicago and produced/hosted a local TV show called *Live a Juicy Life*. Her show was sparked by meeting Oprah Winfrey in November 2006. She has interviewed John Gray, Sonia Choquette and Judith Wright to name a few.

Lilou's '100-Day Reality Challenge':
www.cocreatingourreality.com/profile/lilou

Lilou's YouTube channel:
www.youtube.com/liloumace

ABOUT THE EDITOR

Like Lilou, Dr R Eric Swanepoel has an international background. Born in Edinburgh of a Scottish mother and a South African father, he has lived in Zimbabwe, South Africa, France, and all over the UK. He is now back in Edinburgh. He has worked, amongst other things, as a veterinarian and a teacher of English to speakers of other languages. His doctorate was awarded for studies of pipistrelle bats. He currently works as a part-time researcher in the Scottish Parliament, but says his hobby is playing the fiddle badly and his passion is writing.

He comments, 'I was thrilled when Lilou approached me. I would like to think that I have a talent for helping people tell their stories, but I only work with people whose integrity I admire. I realised from Lilou's YouTube videos that she had something special.

'Given the tight schedule, this project was a challenge. I saw my task as helping Lilou express her unique personality as clearly as possible, and not to impose myself on it in any way. This book is unlike anything else I have worked on. It offers readers the privilege of looking into the evolving thoughts of an honest, courageous and caring human being who lives her "juicy" life 100% on purpose.'

Eric's website: www.BioWrite.co.uk

Eric's blog: BioWrite.wordpress.com